Christ's Soon Return

Christ's Soon Return

The Second Coming of Christ

DAVID E. SEIP

Editor

Preater

An Imprint of Leqach Publishing, Inc. • Langhorne, Pennsylvania

CHRIST'S SOON RETURN
The Second Coming of Christ

Unless otherwise indicated, all Scripture quotations are taken from The King James Version (KJV) Bible: King James Version, public domain.

Leqach Publishing
P.O. Box 1031
Langhorne, PA 19047
www.leqach.com

Cataloging-in-Publication data:

Names: Seip, David E., Editor.

Title: Christ's Soon Return: The Second Coming of Christ | David E. Seip

Description: Langhorne, PA: Leqach Publishing, Inc. 2023

Identifiers: ISBN 978-1-7364043-2-4 (hardback)
ISBN 978-1-7364043-3-1 (paperback) |
ISBN 978-1-7364043-4-8 (ebook)

Subjects: LCSH: Religious Belief | Eschatology |

Library of Congress Control Number: 2023933876
Classifications: BT 826.6 2023 (print) | BT 826.6 (ebook)

Cover design by TSG, Inc.
Cover photo by Tyler Sturos
Manufactured in the U.S.A.   5/2023

For those who long for Christ's appearing

Editor's Preface

Occasionally there is virtually nothing more that can be said on a subject than what has already been historically laid out in writing. We search in vain for a new thread to express our opinion only to find someone has been there before us, and perhaps said it much more astutely. Such is the case before the reader. The topic of this book is the second coming of Christ. There is no topic quite so important to the Christian than the hope of the soon appearing of the Lord Jesus Christ. The Scriptures speak of two comings of Christ—the first to suffer and to grant salvation, the second as the finisher of that salvation. Of the forty-six prophets from Enoch to John, the human author of the Book of Revelation, only six have prophesied of Christ's first coming, but with allusions also of the second, while the remaining forty predicted explicitly his second coming.

There is much that has been written on the subject of Christ's second coming with varying degrees of adroitness and accuracy. Thousands of books have occupied this subject over time. Perhaps the best of the writings may be found in the archival records of the nineteenth century. The early doctors of the faith tackled the subject with not so surprising agreement, but their attention was narrowly focused on the premillennial return of Christ—placing his return at the beginning of that dispensation. Not until later would a debate ensue over the sequence of future events related to Christ's return and the manipulation of Scripture to support the varying positions.

This book assumes the truth of Scripture's progressive revelation to have long settled the matter; and it proposes to wholeheartedly affirm the teaching of Christ's premillennial return. Several authors could have been chosen to lead the reader thoroughly through the Bible's teaching on the Second Coming, but one stands out as most useful. Affirming the extent of what he has written, nothing of any useful explanation need be added. The author is Richard Cunningham Shimeall (1803–1874). Reverend Shimeall was born in New York City, and graduated from the Protestant Episcopal General Theological Seminary in 1824. He first officiated as rector of a Protestant Episcopal church, then changed affiliations to the Reformed Dutch church, and finally to the Presbyterian church—perhaps for reasons associated with his strongly held beliefs on prophecy and millenarianism. He was regarded as a profound biblical scholar, most known for his works on subjects connected with the prophecies and their interpretation. Curiously, of his principal publications, the one presented in this book is not mentioned, nor well known, even though it contains over three hundred pages and was his last major work published prior to his death. It therefore contains the full breadth of his knowledge accumulated over his lifetime on the subject of the end times and Christ's expected return.

Shimeall's work in the pages to follow was originally published in 1873, under the title, *The Second Coming of Christ*.[1] It was written in five comprehensive chapters. We have condensed the chapters into preferable lengths and simplified the sentence structure where possible to allow the reader a more comfortable journey through a scholarly volume which may, at times, otherwise have felt like heavy theological lifting. In Shimeall's own words, he wrote the volume because of the absence of any work which addressed the wants of both the clergy and the laity, and he did so "free of all intricacy." He formed two requisites. First he freed himself from all extraneous matter pertaining to the subject; and second, he purposed to place side-by-side all the theories that have been introduced in the Christian Church from the beginning of the church to the time of his writing. He examined them in the light of Scripture and history while leaving it to the reader—under the guidance of the Holy Spirit—to adopt his own belief.

Shimeall, concerned for his readers who were not conversant with the subject of Christ's second coming in light of the writers who occupied the field of discussion, begins his volume by dividing the discussion into three classes. They are the same three which occupy the discussion today. It will be helpful for some to review the classifications before beginning this book. The first class belongs to those technically called Anti-millenarians, who allege that the Millennium of Revelation 20:1–6 is already past. From this class of writers has originated three distinct theories, which

---

1   R. C. Shimeall, *The Second Coming of Christ; or, The Impending Approach of the "Restitution of All Things" (Acts 3:21) By the "Power and Coming" of The God-Man, "The Lord Jesus Christ." (2 Peter 1:16) Scripturally, Philosophically, and Historically Demonstrated* (New York: Henry S. Goodspeed & Co., Publishers, 1873).

Shimeall will identify in his Preface. The second class is called Post-millenarians, who, though they maintain that the Millennium is still future, yet allege that the second coming of Christ is Post-millennial. The third class is described as Pre-millennialists. This class of writers, while they also hold that the Millennium is still future, affirm that the second coming of Christ takes place before in order to establish the Kingdom of the Son of Man.

In Shimeall's own words: "All we ask of the reader is, that he will 'stand in the way, and see, and ask for the old paths, where is the good way, and walk therein,'" (Jeremiah 6:6), that he may 'find rest for his soul' from the confusion and perplexity so prevalent on this momentous subject. It is always difficult to see through the murky waters of prophecy as explained over time by well-meaning, often learned authors. Opinions relevant to end time events commonly bring the reader to theological despair when attempting to connect the dots of one theorist while overlaying it upon another. What the concerned reader needs more than any other is a gold standard he can rely upon by which to interpret Bible prophecy and its revelation of coming end time events. Shimeall has gifted subsequent generations with such a standard. He traverses time from the early post-apostolic era, compares man's ruminations to Holy Scripture, and furnishes a complete history of the doctrine surrounding Christ's return in order that the reader may traverse his way through the labyrinth of thought and come out the other end with the surest of footing upon the subject.

This edited version of Shimeall's work is divided into two parts—the first part being comprised of the information previously described, and the second part providing an in-depth discussion of the history of millennialism. It is couched in the context of a refutation of the work of William Greenough Thayer Shedd (1820–1894) who wrote on the subject at hand. Shedd was a high Calvinist and one of the most notable systematic theologians of the American Presbyterian church. Nevertheless, Shimeall took disapproval to much of Shedd's conclusions concerning the historical significance of mellenarianism, making his rebuttals and contradictions noteworthy to the reader's comprehension of the subject. Shimeall packs his defense with an extensive display of historical participants—from the early church fathers to those of his day,—and thus brings to light much depth of truth regarding the ebb and flow of predictions about the order and necessity of events surrounding Christ's second coming. The reader is certain to benefit from Shimeall's extensive knowledge.

David E. Seip
Philadelphia, May, 2023

Contents

Editor's Preface | VII

PART ONE
Author's Preface | XVII
Introduction | 1
Chapter 1: Past, Present and Future | 19
Chapter 2: A Premillennial Return | 37
Chapter 3: Prophecy of the Old Testament | 57
Chapter 4: Nature of the Resurrected State | 71
Chapter 5: Evidence of Christ's Glorified Humanity | 97
Chapter 6: Summary of Millenarianism | 121
Chapter 7: Structure of the Millennial Hierarchy | 131

PART TWO
History of Millennialism | 145
Ancient Millenarianism | 147
Early Post Apostolic | 155
Commencement of Apostasy From Ancient Chiliasm | 169
Millenarianism During the Medieval Age | 177
Revival of Modern Millenarianism | 185
Conclusion | 222

PART ONE

Author's Preface

The Creeds, Confessions of Faith, Articles of Religion, and covenants of every branch of the Church throughout Christendom, Roman, Greek, and Protestant, recognize the doctrine of the second coming of the Lord Jesus Christ, in resurrection power, as an undoubted scriptural truth. Nevertheless, from an early period of her history, the Christian Church has been at issue with herself on the great question regarding the nature and purposes of that event, and of the period when it will take place.

The theories which have obtained the greatest notoriety on this subject since the time of Origen (A.D. 204–254), are the following:

1. The first theory is that of Augustine (A.D. 390–430), bishop of Hippo, (advocated also by Primasius, Andreas, Bede), of a spiritual resurrection, which—as this ancient writer followed the computation of the LXX [the Septuagint] for the epoch of the nativity, in other words, in the middle of the sixth chiliad [millennium] of the world's history—he affirms is dated from the first coming of Christ, by whom Satan was wounded, and the strong man disarmed and ejected from the hearts of men—the term of

its continuance to be the remainder of the said sixth chiliad.

2. The second theory is that put forth by Hammond and Grotius, between A.D. 1641 and 1660. These writers allege, that the second coming of Christ consists of an ecclesiastical resurrection, and that it commenced with the opening of the fourth century, continued one thousand literal years, and ended in the fourteenth century.

3. The third theory is that of Daniel Whitby [English theologian and biblical commentator], whose death occurred in 1726. He taught that the resurrection of the martyrs (Revelation 20:4), is to consist of a unique revival of pure Christian principles, the time of which is still future, and is to follow the destruction of Anti-Christ, after which, the whole earth being permeated with these Christian principles, Christ is to commence a spiritual reign over the nations for a thousand years. It is this theory which has formed the basis of the current theology of the Christian Church since his time.

4. This theory, combining those both of Augustine and Whitby as the basis on which it stands, alleges that those prophecies which speak of "the kingdom of heaven," "the kingdom of God," "the kingdom of the Son of Man," as associated with the reign of Christ on earth, refers to the first introduction and establishment of the Christian Church; the dispensation of which, being identical with "the kingdom of heaven" over which Christ reigns by His spirit, merges into, forms a part of, and ends with, the close of the millennial age—at which time Christ is to personally appear, simultaneously raise the dead, both just and unjust, and grant to them rewards and punishments according to their works. This makes the Millennium to be future.

But, in addition to these four theories, and the principles applied in remoulding and amplifying them, there is another.

5. A fifth system, which maintains that the Christian Church and "the kingdom of the Son of Man" are entirely separate and distinct; that there is to be a literal resurrection of departed saints and martyrs to take place at the second personal coming of Christ, before, and in order to, the setting up of the kingdom of Christ, and over which they are to conjointly reign for a thousand years. Also that, during that period, Satan is to be restrained from tempting, harassing, and injuring mankind; and that, at the close of that period, the wicked dead are to be raised and judged (Revelation 20:4, 5).

Now, it is obvious to the plainest mind, that these variant theories, and the principles applied to their explanation, cannot be made to harmonize with the "one faith" as revealed in the inspired word. Indeed, only one of the number can claim to be in accordance with that imputable "faith" at first "delivered to the saints." On this ground, many plead that the truth in this matter lay beyond our reach. In other words, that the prophecies are among those "deep things " of "the mysteries of God's will," which it was never intended to be understood—at least until they are fulfilled. This objection is especially urged against prophetical dating. Mr. Miller [William Miller]and others, it is said, have been mistaken. Therefore, no man living can reach anything definite or reliable regarding them. And that in the face of that positive declaration of the inspired Apostle Peter, that "we have a more sure word of prophecy," respecting which we are admonished that "we all do well to take heed, as unto a light which shines in a dark place, until the day dawn, and the day-star arise in our hearts." (2 Peter 1:13). We are also told that the old prophets "have inquired and searched diligently, who prophesied of the grace that should come unto us; searching what, or what manner of time, the spirit of Christ which was in them signify when it testified beforehand the sufferings of Christ, and the glory that should follow." (1 Peter 1:10, 11). And also of the apocalyptic benediction, " Blessed is he that reads, and they that hear the words of this prophecy, and keep those things which are written therein; for the time is at hand." (Revelation 1:3).

But, we deferentially ask: Do we not otherwise reason in regard to other portions of the equally "deep things" of God's revealed mysteries? All that we now plead for in reference to "the great theological question of the day," that it is a fair subject for candid and open discussion. Why, then, should it be made an exception, as an acknowledged part of the "all Scripture given by inspiration of God?" Surely, because men differ in their views respecting it forms no just grounds as to why it should be ignored. If, for example, the rule for the rejection of a matter of divine revelation is the measure of its misrepresentation, perversion, or abuse, then what becomes of our common Christianity? Try it in its application to the doctrine of the proper deity of Christ, as "God manifest in the flesh"—of the personality and deity of the Holy Spirit, of justification by faith, of perseverance in grace, of future retributions. These, one and all, on the above principle, having each in their turn been alike perverted, opposed, and denied, had been alike erased from the shield of our common Christianity, like a name inscribed upon the sand!

There are few among those who professedly receive the "Scriptures as given by inspiration of God," who are willing to risk their eternal salvation on such an alternative. What? Close our Bibles, obliterate the Sabbath, shut up our churches, annihilate the ministry, and trample the ordinances of our holy religion under foot, in a word, reject Christianity, because, indeed, the variant theories which have risen among men have availed to pervert and abuse them? "The children of this world," in their treatment of the occult sciences, "are wiser in their generation." With them, these have advanced, and continue to advance in the scale of exactitude, just in proportion as they have suffered from the errors and abuses of men. Would we not do well to take an analogous lesson from them?

Let the reader, then, bear in mind, that all misconceptions, perversions, and abuses of scriptural truth, whether of doctrines or of the prophecies, being the result either of ignorance, mere zeal, or open hostility, are to be subjected to the ordeal of God's holy word, which is to "try every man's work, of what sort it is." (1 Corinthians 3:1). Whatever respect we may have for the persons or of confidence in the opinions of the learned, either of the past or the present age, in matters of revealed truth, we can "call no man master." In the words of Chillingworth [William Chillingworth], "The Bible, and the Bible alone, is the religion of Protestants." In the exposition, therefore, of the great and sublime doctrine of the second personal coming of the Lord Jesus Christ, as set forth in this volume, our motto is, "To the law and to the testimony: if we speak not according to this word, it is because there is no light in us." (Isaiah 8:20).

And, although "many have taken in hand to set in order a declaration of those things" which have been so fully revealed in Holy Scripture on this subject, it is nevertheless undeniable, that in the popular theological nomenclature of the day, through both the pulpit and the press, it has either been so sublimated, mystified, etherealized—so mutilated—so confounded with other great acts and purposes of "God in Christ," on the one hand; or so neglected, ignored, or held up to contempt, on the other; that there is a need, to put forth endeavor to rescue it from those prejudices which false theories have created in regard to it. Why: if Bishop Colenso's [John William Colenso] semi-infidel attack upon the inspired Pentateuch of Moses has called forth some four hundred replies in its defense, on both sides of the Atlantic; is it unreasonable that this first attempt to thoroughly canvass the variant and conflicting theories, ancient and modern, on the subject in hand, should be put forth to redeem it from the errors and delusions which have come about in the church? We concede that not a few treatises have appeared, from time to time, especially within the last half century, on both sides of this great theological question of the present day. But, in the judgment of the writer, not one of them has fairly grappled with the difficulties, and met and removed the objections of antagonist writers. Nor can this be accomplished, except by a careful, patient, candid, and thorough examination of the question on its merits, separately from, and independently of, all superfluous and extraneous matters.

In our endeavor, therefore, to restore this glorious doctrine of the Lord's second coming to its proper place in the great firmament of revealed truth—that doctrine which has inspired the faith, nourished the hope, kindled the love, and supported the constancy of the chosen people of God, from the first hour of promised redemption through Christ to the present—we have conducted our examinations of it (in connection with all the theories and principles of interpretation that have appeared, so far as entitled to notice), on the only true basis, that is, of analyzing each theory separately and subjecting it to the threefold test of truth, "scripturally, historically, and philosophically considered." How far we may have succeeded in this endeavor, we leave for the future to determine. Duty is ours; results belong to God.

In conclusion, we have only to add that, adopting as our standpoint that the second personal coming of our Lord is Pre-millennial, we enter our protest against its being confounded with that of modern Millerism. To explain.

1. Millenarians, together with the advocates of the current theology of the Church, and the Millerites, all maintain that the second personal coming of Christ is to take place at the close of that period called in the New Testament (Luke 21:24, and Romans 11:25) "the times of the Gentiles."

2. The circumstance which has led to a confounding of Millenarianism with Millerism, is the proximate nearness of that event, as alleged by both; whereas the advocates of the popular theory, on the hypothesis that "the times of the Gentiles" merge into, form a part, and end at the close of the millennial era, affirm that it takes place after that period. But,

3. Both Millenarians, and the advocates of the popular view, at least for the most part, maintain the existence

on earth of a millennium of blessedness of the saved nations in the flesh for a thousand years.

4. On the contrary, Millerism denies this. The only difference, however, between the theory of Mr. Miller [William Miller]and that of the popularly received view of the Church of the present day is, that, as both place the second personal coming of the Lord at the close of "the times of the Gentiles," Mr. Miller antedated that event, by alleging that it was to occur in 1843, instead of at the end of the thousand years. On all other points, there is an exact correspondence between Millerism and the current view of the Church, in regard to all the events which are to follow the second personal coming of Christ, e.g., the universal conflagration of the earth and the immediate introduction of the human race into their eternal state of bliss or of woe. Again,

5. While, according to the theory of Millerism, time was to close and eternity to begin immediately after 1843; Millenarians, in unison with the advocates of the popular view, maintain that time does not end until the close of the millennial era. Nevertheless,

6. While Millenarians affirm that the second personal coming of Christ is pre-millennial, the prevailing theology of the Church alleges it to be post-millennial. Hence the difference between the two classes of writers as to the nature of Christ's reign over the saved nations in the flesh during the millennium; the former insisting that it is a literal, personal reign; the latter, that it is to consist of a spiritual reign only. It is in place here, therefore, to account for this difference of views on this momentous subject.

We observe, then, that while the remote occasion of it

arises from the different rules of interpretation of the pro-phetic Scriptures, Millenarians adopting the literal, and their opponents the allegorical or spiritual rule; the immediate or direct occasion is that some millenarian writers—prominent among whom is the Rev. Dr. Cumming of London—allege that the second personal coming of Christ not only, but also the universal destruction of the earth, is pre-millennial.

Now, we maintain that this is one among a number of millenarian oddities, which tend to bewilder and confound many sincerely honest and inquiring minds. Indeed, it forms the great stumbling block in the way of an acceptance of the truth in these considerations. Post-Millenarians, for ex-ample, cannot reconcile the above alleged universal destruc-tion of the earth as being pre-millennial, with the fact of the perpetuity of those races of men who are to people the earth during the millennium.

The question, what is to become of them while that process is going on, no Millenarian, on the above hypoth-esis, ever has, or ever can answer. It is a stupendous theo-logical misnomer! The Scriptures clearly teach—as will be shown in the proper place—that the universal destruction is post-millennial. "Convince me of this," says a distinguished post-millenarian clergyman, recently, "and I will adopt the millenarian view, that the second personal coming of Christ is pre-millennial."

It results, therefore, First: That the only difference be-tween the theory of Millerism and the current theology of the Church, on the subject of Christ's second personal coming is, that the latter insists there is to be a millennium before that event takes place.

While, Second: True millenarianism maintains, against

the Millerites, a future millennium of blessedness to the saved nations in the flesh; and against the popular view, that the second personal coming of Christ is not post, but pre-millennial.

The writer has no ambition to be thought "original" in the production of this treatise, beyond what may be conceded of the method adopted in these discussions. While he acknowledges his obligations to both classes of expositors occupying the extensive field over which he has passed, to avoid encumbering his pages with lengthy quotations, he has preferred to adopt his own phraseology, for the most part, in availing himself of any suggestions or facts necessary to his purpose.

May the Holy Spirit guide the inquiring mind into all truth, for Christ's sake.

R.C. Shimeall

New York, January, 1873

Introduction

On the doctrinal part of the subject, our quotations must be limited, for want of space, to the most prominent and pertinent proof texts, only observing that the doctrine of Christ's second coming is not confined to any one part of Scripture. We begin with the Old Testament.

Sir Isaac Newton, who wrote an elaborate work on the prophecies, has well said, that "there is scarcely a prophecy of the Old Testament which does not in something or other relate to the second coming of Christ." Let us apply this remark to the first promise of grace to man—"And I will put enmity between thee (the serpent-tempter) and the woman, and between thy seed and her seed: it (the woman's seed, Christ) shall bruise thy head, and thou shalt bruise his heel." Now, on this passage I observe, that Christ's incarnation of the Virgin Mary by the power of the Holy Ghost, teaches us that He is the woman's promised "seed;" while His crucifixion on the cross was explanatory of the bruising of His heel by satanic power and malice. At the same time the wondrous prodigies present upon the tragic scene of Calvary, "When God the mighty Maker died for man the creature's sin," furnished evidence that He triumphed over the serpent-tempter, by "leading captivity captive, and purchasing gifts for men." This, however, was but the first blow inflicted upon the "head" of the "strong man armed," by the hand of "the stronger than he." His final bruising is reserved for the future. Satan, as "the god of this world," "the prince of the power of the air," still "works in the children of disobedience, leading men," not only individually but also nationally, "captive at his will." The ultimate triumph awaits the incarceration, and the final casting of the serpent in the lake of fire, both of which acts are future, and are to be consummated at the period of the second coming of Christ.

The next prophecy of this event is that of Enoch, as recorded by the Apostle Jude. "And Enoch, the seventh from Adam, prophesied of these, saying, Behold, the Lord cometh with ten thousand of his saints, to execute judgment upon all." Christ's first coming was on an errand of mercy. It announced the offer of peace on earth, and of good will to man." But, at His second coming, though, "to them who look for him, he will appear the second time without sin unto salvation;" yet, man's probationary economy under the gospel dispensation having then closed, He will pour out the libations of His wrath upon the impenitent and incorrigible despiser of His word. The fact that His first coming was not accompanied with "ten thousand of his saints," is decisive proof that Enoch's prophecy refers to His second coming.

The same holds true of the "Prophet" predicted by Moses, to whom the people should "listen." (Deuteronomy 18:15). Also of the "Shiloh" of Jacob, unto whom "the gathering of the people should be." The same of the "Star" of Balaam, who was to "rise out of Jacob and have dominion." Now, though these several prophecies related primarily to the first coming of Christ, yet neither of them was fully verified by that event. For, of the first, our blessed Lord, as the great prophetic "Teacher sent from God," complained of the people, "Ye will not come unto me, that ye might have life." But, a predicted period never yet realized will come, when "neighbor will no more say to neighbor, know ye the Lord; but when all shall know him from the least to the greatest." So of the second. After all the gatherings to Christ that have taken place out of all the nations of the earth for more than eighteen hundred years, it has been, and still is, true of the church that she remains emphatically a "little flock." But it is predicted of her that "in the last days, the mountain of the Lord's house shall be established in the top of the mountains, and shall be exalted above the hills," and that then "all nations shall flow unto it." No one will pretend that this universal in-gathering to Christ has ever yet been fulfilled. And so of the third. The "Star" Christ, that arose out of Jacob at the first coming, so far from then having the "dominion" predicted of him, was "cast out and killed," as the rightful "heir," and his inheritance seized by his murderers. But it is predicted of him that he shall reign, and his dominion shall extend from sea to sea, and from the rivers to the ends of the earth. These latter predictions, therefore, not having been fully verified by the events of the first, must depend upon and await the second coming of Christ.

I pass on to the remarkable prophecy of Job, respecting this event, in the following words: "I know that my Redeemer liveth, and that he shall stand at the latter day upon the earth: and though, after my skin worms destroy this body, yet in my flesh shall I see God; whom I shall see for myself, and mine eyes shall behold, and not another; though my reins be consumed within me." There are not a few in the school of modern biblical critics, who affirm that this passage of Job is to be understood simply of that change in his experience, from a state of adversity and bodily suffering, to that of his restoration to redoubled prosperity and blessing, in this life; an hypothesis founded upon the words, "as the cloud is consumed and vanisheth away; so he that goeth down to the grave shall come up no more." Also, "If a man die, shall he live again?" And again, "When a few years are come, then shall I go the way whence I shall not return." It is alleged by these writers, that Job was totally ignorant both of the doctrine of man's immortality and of a future resurrection; and therefore that this passage can have no reference to the future second coming of Christ. The fallacy of this hypothesis, however, is sufficiently obvious from Job's words when speaking of the dead, "He shall return no more to his house, neither shall his place know him any more." That is, all his relations with this life are ended forever, equivalent to the passage, "if the tree fall towards the south, or towards the north, in the place where the tree falleth, there it shall be."

Again. That Job was at least no less acquainted with the doctrine of man's immortality and of the resurrection of the dead at the last day, as connected with, and dependent upon, the second coming of Christ, than those of Enoch, and Moses, and Jacob is clear from the sense in which this passage is understood by the Jewish rabbis. Mr. C.W.H. Pauli, in his "Analecta Hebraiaca," having rendered the clause in the 25th verse, "And he that is the Last (the Christ) shall stand upon the dust," i.e., the earth; in opposition to the above perversion of its true meaning, says: "I rendered "the latter day," *He that is the Last*, not only because I am fully convinced from the whole context that Job meant to say to his friends, 'I do not look for any deliverance at your hands, but my hopes are fixed upon Him, who is the resurrection and the life;' but also the ancient rabbis have taken this word in the sense of God."

We now pass to the Psalms of David, in which this great event is frequently set forth in the most emphatic and glowing terms. The following, as an example, must suffice: "Our God shall come, and shall not keep silence: a fire shall devour before him, and it shall be very tempestuous round about him. He shall call to the heavens from above, and to the earth, that he may judge his people."

The next inspired witnesses to this same truth, are the old prophets, whose predictions regarding it are so numerous, and announced on such a variety of occasions, that I must content myself to group together only a small portion of them, with little or no comment.

I commence with the following from Isaiah. "And there shall come forth a Rod out of the stem of Jesse, and a Branch shall grow out of his roots...which shall stand as an ensign of the people: to it shall the Gentiles seek; and His rest shall be glorious." It will require but a cursory glance at the context, to perceive that this prophecy relates exclusively to the second coming of Christ, to "smite the earth with the rod of his mouth, and with the breath of his lips to slay the wicked;" "and to fill the earth with the knowledge of the Lord, as the waters cover the sea."

Jeremiah repeats the same prophecy: "Behold, the days

come, saith the Lord, that I will raise unto David a righteous Branch, and a king shall reign and prosper, and shall execute judgment and justice in the earth. In his days Judah shall be saved, and Israel shall dwell safely: and this is his name whereby he shall be called, THE LORD OUR RIGHTEOUSNESS." At the first appearing, our blessed Lord, so far from realizing the things here predicted of Him, was rejected as a king, and was crucified by the Jews, which resulted in the overthrow of their civil and ecclesiastical government, the destruction of their city and temple, and their dispersion among all nations, where with the Ten Tribes were in exile. This prophecy, therefore, must be prospective of Christ's return from heaven.

Ezekiel refers to the same event in that beautiful passage, "Behold, the glory of the God of Israel came from the way of the east; and his voice was like the voice of many waters: and the earth shined with his glory." Totally unlike this, His first coming: such was then the humiliation of the Incarnate Word, that, "as a tender plant, and a root out of a dry ground," when seen, he was adjudged to have neither "comeliness nor beauty," to attract the eye. "He was oppressed and afflicted, yet he opened not his mouth. He was brought as a lamb to the slaughter." The sun refused to look upon the deed! "From the sixth hour there was darkness over all the earth unto the ninth hour."

The next testimony is given in the words of Daniel, which, for vastness of conception and boldness of imagery, well fits the theme. "I saw in the night visions, and behold, one like the Son of Man came with the clouds of heaven, and came to the ancient of days, and they brought him near before him. And there was given him dominion, and glory, and a kingdom, that all people, nations, and languages should serve him."

Joel prolongs the same theme, as follows: "The sun and the moon shall be darkened, and the stars shall withdraw their shining. The Lord also shall roar out of Zion, and utter his voice from Jerusalem, and the heavens and the earth shall shake; but the Lord will be the hope of his people, and the strength of the children of Israel."

Corresponding with this prophecy of the Lord's second coming is the following from Haggai. "Yet once, saith the Lord of hosts, it is a little while, and I will shake the heavens and the earth, and the dry land. And I will shake all nations, and the Desire of all nations (the Christ) shall come."

And to this the prophet Zechariah he responds: "And the Lord my God shall come, and all his saints with him."..."And his feet shall stand in that day upon the mount of Olives which is before Jerusalem."

Finally, to the above, Malachi adds the last link to this golden chain of prophetic testimony in the Old Testament to this great truth. He says: "For, behold, the day cometh that shall burn as an oven; and all the proud, yea, and all the wicked shall be as stubble...But unto you that fear my name shall the sun of righteousness arise with healing in his wings." "For the Lord whom ye seek, shall suddenly come to His temple, even the messenger of the covenant whom ye delight in: Behold He shall come, saith the Lord of hosts." Now, in whatever sense this prophecy may be applied to the circumstances of the first coming of Christ, it cannot be maintained that it was verified in all its parts. Christ came not then to "destroy men's lives," but "to seek and to save them that were lost." Neither did men then "delight" in him. For, being "not sent but unto the lost sheep of the house of Israel," we read that "He came unto his own, but His own received Him not." Nor did his own followers then "go forth, and grow up, and become as calves of the stall." For they were all "scattered, as sheep having no shepherd." It must, therefore, have an ulterior reference to that day of which the prophet speaks when he says, "But who may abide the day of His coming? And who shall stand when He appeareth? For he is like a refiner's fire, and like fuller's soap:" even that day when, with the winnowing "fan in his hand, He will thoroughly purge his floor, and gather the wheat into his storehouse."

We pass now to the New Testament. Here, the light of prophecy on this momentous subject is reflected with a greatly augmented brightness. We open this testimony with the angelic announcement respecting the Son of God, as the Son of Mary, in these memorable words: "He shall be great, and shall be called the Son of the Highest: and the Lord God shall give unto Him the throne of His father David: and He shall reign over the house of Israel forever; and of His kingdom there shall be no end!" It is here to be observed, that, inasmuch as there was nothing connected with our Lord's humiliation in the flesh, which could possibly meet the terms of this prophecy concerning him, we are compelled to apply it to that of his predicted "glory which was to follow" his "sufferings," when He should be "revealed from heaven in flaming fire with His mighty angels, to take vengeance on them that know not God, and that obey not the gospel;" and when, "wearing His many crowns," and seated on His father David's throne, "the kingdom, and dominion, and greatness of the kingdom under the whole heaven should be given to him" and to his "saints."

We quote a second angelic prediction of this event. "And while they (i.e., the disciples of Galilee) looked steadfastly toward heaven as He went up, behold, two men stood by them in white apparel; who also said, Ye men of Galilee, why stand ye gazing up into heaven? This same Jesus which is taken up from you into heaven, shall so come in like manner as ye see Him go into heaven." But, let us see what Christ Himself said, concerning this doctrine. A little prior to His crucifixion, with a view to console His desponding disciples in the prospect of His separation from them, He said: "Let not your hearts be troubled: ye believe in God, believe also in me. In my Father's house are many mansions:"..."and I go to prepare a place for you, and if I go and prepare a place for you, I will come again, and receive you unto myself: that where I am, there ye may be also."

On another occasion Jesus said to the Jews, seeing that they still persevered in rejecting Him as their Messiah, "Behold, your house is left unto you desolate"—a prediction this, of the overthrow of their government and the destruction of their city and temple by the Roman legions—to which He adds, "For I say unto you, ye shall not see me henceforth, till ye shall say, Blessed is He that cometh in the name of the Lord." Here our blessed Lord refers, though indefinitely, to the time of His "return" from heaven, where He was going to prepare those "many mansions" for His faithful followers, spoken of in the last preceding passage.

Again. By way of correcting an error into which His disciples had fallen, as though the Messianic kingdom was then to be restored to them; Jesus predicts that a long interval would ensue, between His ascension and His coming again. "He said unto His disciples, The days will come, when ye shall desire to see one of the days of the Son of Man, and ye shall not see it." That is, they should not see it according to their expectation of it: not that they should never witness it. For, He proceeds to notify them of a "sign," which should indicate when it was about to take place. He says: "As the lightning that lighteneth out of one part under heaven, shineth unto another part under heaven, so shall also the Son of Man be in His day." It was on this ground also that, after His resurrection, being asked by His disciples, "Lord, wilt thou at this time restore the kingdom to Israel?" He said, "it is not for you," that is, those of this generation, "to know the times or the seasons, which the Father hath put in his own power." Not that these "times and seasons" should never be revealed. The veil of obscurity then thrown over them, should be withdrawn at the proper time—"the time of the end." That "time" having come, the celestial "sign"—the "lightning" in the heavens—should indicate to all the tribes of the earth, the approaching fulfillment of what He had said,—"They shall see the Son of Man coming in the clouds of heaven, with power and great glory."

But, in addition to the above prophecies of Christ respecting His second coming, and especially as we find that event elaborated in the 24th chapter of Matthew, the 13th chapter of Mark, and the 21st chapter of Luke, the same great truth is set forth in those parables, which form a continuation of that sublime discourse; for example, the parable of the Chief Servant, Matthew 24:45–51. In the case of his unwatchfulness and improper behavior, if found saying "in his heart, my lord delayeth his coming," we are told that "the lord of that servant shall come in a day when he looketh not for him, and in an hour that he is not aware of; and shall cut him asunder, and appoint his portion with the hypocrites: there shall be weeping and gnashing of teeth." (verses 50, 51).

So also the illustrative parable of the ten virgins, Matthew 25:1–13. In it is taught the necessity of being in readiness for the coming of the Lord to receive His people into his presence and glory. Hence the enforcement of the admonition, "Watch, therefore, for ye know neither the day nor the hour wherein the Son of Man cometh." Moreover, in this parable, the midnight cry is heard, "Behold, the Bridegroom cometh!" It is in this character that our Lord is represented as coming at the last day, in the Apocalypse [the book of Revelation], chapter 19:7–9. The termination of the day of offered grace, and the final separation, at the judgment of the living nations, between the just and the unjust, are graphically delineated in the sequel of the parable.

To these may be added the parable of the talents delivered to the servants, Matthew 25:14–30. In it we have an illustration of the Lord's personal withdrawal from his servants, after giving them their charge (verse 15); then, "after a long time," of His return to account with them: i.e., to bring them to judgment; when, to the faithful, there is the reward, by exalting them to dominion (verse 23), and their admission to the joy of their Lord: to the unfaithful, punishment, denoted by the casting of the unprofitable servant into outer darkness (verse 30). The parable of the noble man who distributes among his servants ten pounds, and takes his "journey into a far country to receive a kingdom and to return," is of similar meaning, only that it brings more fully into view than in the other, the design of Christ's personal absence from the Church during the interval from His ascension to His second coming, namely, to await His full honor of His kingly prerogatives, as the pre-ordained PRINCE OF THE KINGS OF THE EARTH.

We shall now conclude this golden chain of testimony to the doctrine of Christ's second coming by passing on to the epistles, that we may ascertain what the inspired Apostles taught on this subject. It is of the first importance here to observe, that what our blessed Lord, as above, had predicted of this event, "formed the great textbook from which the Apostles and primitive Christians mainly derived, not only their doctrines, but their illustrations, of the second coming of Christ, and the destinies of men that shall result!" And thus was fulfilled our Lord's avowed intention of keeping his words before the Church in all ages: "And what I say I say unto all, watch!"

The Apostles Paul and Peter, and James and Jude, and John, as the writers of the Holy Spirit in perpetuating the doctrine of the Lord's second coming, speak of it in every variety of form that is calculated to focus attention, and to keep alive in the Church a spirit of prayer, and watchfulness, and patient waiting for that event. And, mark: they all treated it as the foundation of the hope of "eternal life," from the beginning. In expectation of their admission to an "inheritance incorruptible, and undefiled, and that fadeth not away" at the Lord's second appearing, believers are spoken of as "waiting for the Son of God from heaven," and as "loving that appearing." Yes, with the eye of faith fixed on Christ the Coming One, not only in His suffering, but in His glorified humanity, they were strengthened to endure "trial of cruel mockings and scourgings, and moreover, of bonds and imprisonments; and also to be stoned, and sawn asunder, and tempted: to be slain with the sword, to wander about in sheep skins and goat skins, being destitute, afflicted, tormented: also to wander about in deserts, and in mountains, and in dens and caves of the earth." (Hebrews 11:36–38). "Walking by faith and not by sight as seeing Him who is invisible," they had their "conversation [citizenship] in heaven, where they also looked for the Savior, the Lord Jesus Christ, who," when He comes, "shall change our vile body, and fashion it like unto His own glorious body, according to the working whereby He is able to subdue all things to Himself."

Hence the Apostle Paul, having said, in 1 Thessalonians 4:16, "For the Lord HIMSELF shall descend from heaven with a shout, with the voice of archangel, and with the trump of God," continues his discourse on the subject of Christ's judgment-coming as to its results, first, in the punishment of the wicked, thus: "And to you who are troubled, rest with us, when the Lord Jesus shall be revealed from heaven with his mighty angels, in flaming fire, taking vengeance on them that know not God, and that obey not the Gospel of our Lord Jesus Christ: who shall be punished with everlasting destruction from the presence of the Lord, and from the glory of His power " (2 Thessalonians 1:7–9): and second, in the reward of his suffering and faithful followers, by the resurrection of those who sleep in Him, and the rapture of the living saints. His words are: "And the dead in Christ shall rise first:" to which he adds, "Then we which are alive and remain, shall be caught up together with them in the clouds, to meet the Lord in the air; and so shall we ever be with the Lord." (1 Thessalonians 4:16, 17). And finally, third, in regard to this doctrine of the Lord's second coming, he tells his Thessalonian brethren, 1 Thessalonians 5:1–5, "But, of the times and seasons, brethren, ye have no need that I write unto you. For yourselves know perfectly, that the day of the Lord so cometh as a thief in the night. For when they"—i.e., the scoffers of the last days, who, as Peter predicted of them, shall exclaim, "Where is the promise of His coming?"—"when they shall say, Peace and safety: then sudden destruction shall come upon them, as travail upon a woman with child, and they shall not escape." And he again adds: "But ye, brethren, are not in darkness, that that day should overtake you as a thief. Ye are the children of light, and of the day: we are not of the night, nor of darkness."

We ask, therefore, When was it that these Thessalonian brethren "knew perfectly, that the day of the Lord's" coming to raise the dead and change the living saints, "would so come as a thief in the night?" There is no intimation whatever, that they learned it from Paul, or from any of the other apostles. All the epistles, from 1 Corinthians to the Apocalypse inclusive, were written subsequently to our Lord's repeated and varied declarations and illustrations of this sublime subject.

They, therefore only take up and prolong the theme so largely spoken of by the old prophets, and also by Him who "spake as never man spake."

On the general subject of the testimony of the New Testament to this doctrine, it may not be out of place here to observe that, paradoxical as it may appear, it is no less a cause of lamentation than of surprise, that the circumstance of the frequency of its occurrence seems but to weaken the impression that it was designed to produce. Such a result, surely, can only be accounted for, on the ground of the ascendancy of the worldly, over the spiritual life, of the Church. Long exemption from being called to suffer for Christ's sake, has almost totally crushed out that spirit of hope after things heavenly,—in other words, of a readiness to be "crucified to the world with its affections and lusts,"—which characterized the Church of primitive and of later times. Hence the loss, to the Church of this day, for the most part, of a Scriptural view and appreciation of this doctrine, as the foundation of her faith and hope. In the endeavor, therefore, to recover the Church to an acceptance of this fundamental article of "the faith once delivered to the saints," we propose to reproduce, in a condensed form, a few of the many expressions under which this doctrine is represented in the Gospels and Epistles. To this end, we shall group them together under the following heads.

I. "The presence of Christ,"—2 Peter 1:16: "For we have not followed cunningly devised fables when we made known unto you the power and coming of our Lord Jesus Christ, but were eye-witnesses of his majesty." This passage relates to Christ's transfiguration on the mount, as recorded in Matthew 17:2–5; Mark 9:1–7. But, though it transpired during the period of the first coming of Christ, it was but the type and earnest of the glory of the second. Again. To the question of the disciples, "What shall be the sign of thy coming?" (Matthew 24:3), Christ replied, "As the days of Noah were, so shall also the coming of the Son of Man be"(verses 37, 39). The Apostle James said, "Be ye also patient, brethren, establish your hearts: for the coming of the Lord draweth nigh" (chapter 5:7–9). So the Apostle Paul: "Now we beseech you, brethren, by the coming of our Lord Jesus Christ, and by our gathering together unto Him, that ye be not soon shaken in mind." For, "that wicked...the man of sin and son of perdition...shall be revealed, whom the Lord shall consume with the spirit of His mouth, and shall destroy" (i.e., after the example of His transfiguration) "with the brightness of His coming." (2 Thessalonians 2:1–8). See also 1st Thessalonians 1and 2, at various places. The Apostle Peter also speaks of "looking for and hasting unto the coming of the day of God, wherein the heavens being on fire, shall be dissolved," (2 Peter 3:12). And again the Apostle Paul: "But every man in his own order; Christ the first fruits: afterward they that are Christ's at His coming." (1 Corinthians 15:23).

II. His "appearance," or "Epiphany,"—1 Timothy 6:14: "That thou keep this commandment without spot, unrebukable, until the appearing of our Lord Jesus Christ." 2 Timothy 4:8: "Henceforth there is laid up for me a crown of righteousness, which the Lord, the righteous Judge, shall give me at that day; and not to me only, but unto all them also that love His appearing."

III. "Christ's coming,"—Matthew 16:28: "Verily, I say unto you, there be some standing here, which shall not taste of death, till they shall see the Son of Man coming in His kingdom." This "kingdom," however, in its full manifestation, was not in their day restored to them. But they were to be the eye-witnesses of it in its type and earnest, which occurred about six days after on the mount of transfiguration. (Matthew 17:1, 2; Luke 16:26) "For whosoever shall be ashamed of me and of my words, of him shall the Son of Man be ashamed, when He shall come in His own glory." Luke 21:27: "And then shall they see the Son of Man coming in the clouds of heaven with power and great glory." Acts 1:2: "This same Jesus, which is taken up from you into heaven, shall so come in like manner, as ye have seen Him go into heaven." Zechariah 14:5: "And the Lord my God shall come, and all the saints with thee." Malachi 3:1: "And the Lord, whom ye seek, shall suddenly come to His temple." The Apostle Paul, 1 Corinthians 11:26, connects this doctrine with the solemn commemoration of the sufferings and death of Christ in the Lord's Supper: "For as oft as ye eat this bread, and drink this cup, ye do show the Lord's death till He come."

IV. "The day of Christ,"—1 Corinthians 1:8: "Who shall also confirm you unto the end, that ye may be blameless in the day of our Lord Jesus Christ." 2 Corinthians 1:14: "As also ye have acknowledged us in part, that we are your rejoicing, even as ye also are ours in the day of the Lord Jesus." 2 Peter 3:10: "But the day of the Lord will so come as a thief in the night." Philippians 2:16: "Holding forth the word of life; that I may rejoice in the day of Christ, that I have not run in vain, neither labored in vain." Joel 2:31: "The sun shall be turned into darkness, and the moon into blood, before the great and terrible day of the Lord come."

V. "The end,"—"And this gospel of the kingdom shall be preached in all the world for a witness unto all nations, and then shall the end come."

VI. "The close of the age," or "Dispensation,"—"Lo, I am with you alway, even unto the end of the world." (Matthew 28:20) "The harvest is the end of the world: and the reapers are the angels. As therefore the tares are gathered and burned in the fire; so shall it be in the end of this world." (Matthew 13:39, 40, 49).

VII. "Christ made manifest,"—"When Christ, who is our life, shall appear, then shall ye also appear with him in glory." (Colossians 3:4). "And when the Chief Shepherd shall appear, ye shall receive a crown of glory that fadeth not away." (1 Peter 5:4). "Beloved, now are we the sons of God, and it doth not yet appear what we shall be: but we know that, when He shall appear, we shall be like Him, for we shall see Him as He is." (1 John 3:2).

VIII. "Christ revealed"—1 Peter 1:5: "Who are kept by the power of God through faith unto salvation, ready to be revealed in the last time." (See also verse 7). 1 Peter 4:13: "But rejoice, inasmuch as ye are partakers of Christ's sufferings; that, when His glory shall be revealed, ye may be glad also with exceeding joy."

We conclude this presentation of the evidence in support of the doctrine of the Lord's second coming, with the remark, that an event, so extensively and variously exhibited to our view in the scriptures of the Old and New Testaments, could not but have been designed as a subject of frequent, prayerful, and solemn meditation by the church and people of God in all ages. And especially does this hold true of those who, in the dispensations of God's providence and grace, shall be found upon the earth at "the time of the end," when the great "mystery of God," as involved then, is about to be "finished."

How then, I ask, can any who willfully close their minds to this truth, avoid incurring the guilt, and its attendant penalty, of those who "take away from the words of the prophecy of this book," either by overlooking, or perverting, or denying it? Surely, God, in retributive justice, "will take away his part out of the book of life, and out of the holy city, and from the things which are written in this book:" wherein, besides that in every chapter of Paul's two epistles to the Thessalonians, the theme of the Lord's second coming is at least once introduced, the attentive reader of the Revelation will find that, from its beginning to the end, it is constantly presented to view as the one great hope and consolation of the church, in all her appointed pilgrimage;—like an heavenly beacon, it cheers her on through the impending storm; like a glimpse to the laboring mariner of the peaceful haven in the distance, she is constantly encouraged through faith "to lift up the hands that hang down, and the feeble knees." (Hebrews 12:13).

Thus, we see that while a Savior to come in His glory was held up to the faith and hope of the Old Testament saints, before He personally "appeared to put away sin by the sacrifice of Himself" on the cross; the same faith in and hope of His return from heaven in the clouds with power and great glory, both before and after His ascension, were set before the church by Christ and His inspired apostles, with additional luster and distinctness of utterance. And, with this evidence before us in support of the abstract doctrine of the second coming of Christ, we pass to consider it in its practical aspect.

CHAPTER 1

Past, Present, Future

We now enter upon a discussion of the topics connected with this important branch of the subject in hand. This embraces an examination of the question: Will the second coming of Christ consist of an allegorical or spiritual coming, or will it consist of a literally corporeal or personal coming and involving along with it the question: Is that event to be pre- or post-millennial?

We take issue with the advocates of the idea of a kingdom involving the presence and reign of a king; so, throughout the prolonged period of "the times of the Gentiles" onward to the end of the millennium, they insist that Christ has reigned, and that He will continue to reign over His Church, Christian and millennial, after an invisible or spiritual manner; and hence affirm that His second personal coming will be post-millennial.

This is a subject of momentous import. It involves a correct interpretation and application of all those prophecies of the Old and New Testaments in connection with the phraseology, "the kingdom of God;" "the kingdom of heaven;" "the kingdom of the Son of Man." The question regarding them is this: Are the phrases, "the kingdom of God," etc., and the Christian Church, or "Church of God," used interchangeably in the Scriptures to denote the same thing? We answer emphatically, they are not. True, they may exist in alliance with each other, but are nevertheless entirely separate and distinct. Where such a union exists in its purest and most perfect form, as under and during the original theocracy of Israel, the kingdom, with its sovereign, administers laws to, governs, and protects the Church, as its loyal subjects. But, if they revolt against their sovereign, and drive him into exile, and set up a usurper in his place, while the Church continues to exist, the original theocracy, for the time, ceases to be, until it is again restored. Thus it was with Israel in the time of Samuel, when she gave up the theocracy and set up an earth-born rival in the place of God. Hence, He says to Samuel, "they have not rejected thee, but they have rejected me, that I should not be king over them." Hence, too, though "God gave them a king in his anger," Saul, "and took him away in his wrath," and caused David to be anointed in his place, and appointed a succession of kings in the line of descent from him, that arrangement was not a restoration of the original theocracy; but, David being of the tribe of Judah, the design of it was, to lay a foundation to that end, to be accomplished in due time in the person of David's royal son, THE MESSIAH.

And so, when John the Baptist entered upon his mission as the announcer of the Messiah, he found the Jewish nation politically owing to the Roman power. To the Jews he preached, "Repent ye, for the kingdom of heaven," or the restoration of the original theocracy, "is at hand." Also, our blessed Lord, on entering upon His public ministry, presented Himself to the same Church, and took up the same theme with that of John, "Repent ye, for the kingdom of heaven is at hand." And, more, He actually declared Himself to be their King, the long-expected Messiah. And the nation being thrown upon their own responsibility in accepting Him, the Messiah would have then restored the original theocracy to them. It was their duty to have done so; just on the same principle that it is the duty of every man to render perfect obedience to the law of God. But, as in this latter case, so with them. As "the carnal mind is enmity against God, is not subject to his law, neither indeed can be:" so we read, though Messiah "came to his own" world, "yet his own" people, the Jews, "received Him not," but rejected and crucified Him!

We see, then, from this, that during the personal ministry of Christ at His first advent to the Jewish nation, the original theocracy, or "kingdom of God," was not then restored. Still, the Church did not cease to exist. But, it may be asked, was not "the kingdom of God" restored or "set up" immediately after the ascension of our Lord, and if so, does not this make it certain that "the kingdom of God," or of "heaven," and the Christian Church, are one and the same?

This is the popularly received view of the Christian Church of this day. The prevailing theory on this subject is, that "the kingdom of God," or the Church, is a spiritual establishment. And this on the ground, that our blessed Lord declared to the unbelieving Jewish nation that "the kingdom of God should be taken from them, and be given to a people" (the Gentiles) who should "bring forth the fruits thereof." Also that the Apostle Paul said to them, "Seeing ye put these things from you, and judge yourselves unworthy of everlasting life, lo, we turn to the Gentiles." The objection amounts, in other words, to the assertion, "that Christ is now reigning as king in His own proper kingdom; and that this kingdom formally commenced on His ascension to the right hand of God, and that it will continue unchanged, both in character and form, till the end of the millennial age." In support of this theory, we are reminded that Christ and his apostles spoke of the "kingdom of God" or of "heaven" as at hand; as about to be established; and that the apostles, immediately after Christ's ascension, represent it as actually set up.

A formidable array of objections these, to the views we have advocated of "the kingdom of heaven" as still future! The importance of the subject will require an examination into the meaning of the principal passages resorted to by our opponents in the support of their theory.

And here permit me to explain, in the outset, that we by no means object to the sentiment so generally expressed, so to speak, in the sermons and psalmody throughout Christendom, that "Christ reigns in the hearts of his believing people." Undoubtedly He does; but the figurative use of the word "reign," in such an application of it as this, is no authority for displacing the true, scriptural doctrine of Christ's kingdom, as contradistinguished from that church state under this dispensation, into which the predestined subjects of it are "gathered out of (or from among) the Gentiles," and prepared spiritually for their final admission into it as future.

Hence, the present church state is called in the New

Testament "the kingdom of heaven in mystery;" that is, it is that period during which God by his Spirit effectually calls, and enlightens, and regenerates, and justifies, and sanctifies his chosen people, in order to render them ready for their ultimate introduction into the everlasting kingdom of our Lord and Savior Jesus Christ, at its manifestation. Thus Paul says: "For the earnest expectation of the creature waiteth for the manifestation of the sons of God...And not only they, but ourselves also, which have the first-fruits of the spirit, even we ourselves groan within ourselves, waiting for the adoption, to wit, the redemption of our body." This, of itself, might be taken as decisive of the point at issue; for it teaches us that it is only in resurrection that the Church is to be admitted to the possession of the kingdom. No, it is not Christ personally, but it is the Divine Paraclete, the "Comforter," the Holy Spirit, dispensed by Him to the Church on the day of Pentecost, who now "reigns" in the hearts of believers. Christ is now personally absent from the Church; nor, until He "comes again" according to His promise to receive her to himself, can He "reign" over her in His kingdom. An examination into the meaning of the passages already alluded to, will be found to confirm this view.

1. The first passage alleged in proof that the Church in its present state constitutes the spiritual kingdom over which Christ is said to "reign," is the following, John 18:36: "My kingdom is not of this world: if my kingdom were of this world, then would my servants fight, that I should not be delivered to the Jews: but now is my kingdom not from hence."

The difficulty in understanding this passage lies in the

Greek words *kosmos* (world) and *nun* (now). The *kosmos* (world) here, evidently means the aggregate population of the earth. But, there is another Greek word mistranslated "world," viz., *aion*, in the passage, "Lo, I am with you alway, even unto the end of the (*aion*) world." It should have been age or dispensation.

Thus, *kosmos* refers to the people; *aion*, to the age, or period of time, when the people lived. The passage in question was Christ's reply to Pilate, "Art thou the king of the Jews?" And when our Lord said, "My kingdom is not of this world," and also added, "but now is my kingdom not from hence;" and Pilate asked him the second time, "Art thou a king, then?" Jesus answered him, "Thou sayest that I am a king;" that is, it is so; I am a king: "to this end was I born, and for this cause came I into the (*kosmos*) world," i.e., to the Jewish and Gentile world, "that I should bear witness unto the truth." And, for this reason, as Peter and John declared, "both Herod and Pontius Pilate, with the Gentiles, and the people of Israel," conspired to put him to death. Proof that "His kingdom was not of this world,"— not only, that is, it is not composed of men (the collective body of mankind) now dwelling on the earth; for if this were so, "then would my servants fight, that I should not be delivered to the Jews;" but, as "My kingdom is not now from hence,"—that is, does not now take its commencement from hence, or from this point of time, it is still future. In a word, it is as though Christ had said to Pilate, "My kingdom is not" of the "generation of vipers," Jewish and Gentile, of this age: nevertheless, though not of this *kosmos*, it will be on this earth, agreeably to the declaration of Daniel, chapter 7:27, that the kingdom of Messiah, when "set up," will be "under the whole heaven;" and also of the Apostle John, Revelation 11:15, that the kingdoms of this (*kosmos*) world are (or will) become the kingdom of our Lord and of his Christ." We pass to another passage.

2. "The kingdom of God is *within* you." Positive evidence, it is alleged, that Christ's spiritual kingdom, the Church, then existed; or how could it be said to have been "within" those whom he addressed? But who were these? Not his disciples, but the Pharisees. And was it "within" them that this spiritual kingdom was set up? If this is so, then it follows, that Joseph of Arimathea, who was at this very time "waiting for the kingdom of God," was without this inward grace! To escape this dilemma, several eminent writers render *entos humon*, not within, but *among* you. But, that our Lord was not speaking of his kingdom as then present, but *future*, is evident from the fact that he speaks here of two events which must take place before his kingdom could be established. The first was, that he must "suffer many things, and be rejected of that generation;" and the second, that His future personal advent would be preceded, "not with observation," or that fixed, attentive, and prolonged expectation of a coming event of which we know nothing as to either how or where, whether at Bethlehem, Jerusalem, or Galilee; but, "as the lightning that lighteneth out of one part under heaven shineth unto another part under heaven, so should the coming of the Son of Man be." That is, it shall be both instantaneous and irresistible. Then, in the next place,

3. We are referred to that class of passages which speak of Christ's kingdom as "nigh at hand"—"even at the doors." Granted. But this is equally true of other events,

e.g., "The Lord is at hand"—"The coming of the Lord draweth nigh"—"The end of all things is at hand," which all Christians admit and know are still future. And, as there can be no kingdom without a king, it follows, that as Christ has not yet returned, "the kingdom" has not yet been "set up."

4. But, we are also reminded of other passages which speak of Christ's kingdom, as about to be established, that is, during the apostolic age. Such as, the declaration of the angel to Mary: "And the Lord God shall give unto Him (Christ) the throne of His father David." To this we reply, first, that the above angelic prophecy applies to the popular notion of Christ's kingdom as being spiritual; for, during the time of Christ and his apostles, the Davidic throne was a delegated earthly monarchy. Besides, it had been, and was then, utterly supplanted by the Roman Caesars. But second, Jehovah had made an oath to David, that He would raise up his seed after him, that is, Messiah, to sit upon his throne, which should be established forevermore. Hence David, being a prophet, in view of the oath made to him, "that of the fruit of his loins according to the flesh, God would raise up Christ to sit on his throne, he spake of the resurrection of Christ." But third, the Davidic throne as above was not restored immediately after the resurrection. For Christ, after forty days, ascended to heaven, and sat down on His Father's throne, whither "David is not yet ascended." No, brethren, David's throne is still "fallen down;" nor will it be re-erected, until Christ returns from heaven, wearing His "many crowns."

5. Another alleged passage to the same end, is that wherein Christ says to his disciples, "There be some standing

here which shall not taste of death, till they have seen the kingdom of God come with power." This, our opponents affirm, was verified by the descent of the Holy Spirit upon the assembled disciples on the day of Pentecost, when, they say, the spiritual "kingdom of Christ," or the Church, was established. Again we repeat: No, brethren, the Church existed before. That event was a fulfilment of the promise of Christ to his disconsolate disciples when He was about to leave them: "I will send you another comforter...even the Spirit of truth." And this, in accordance with the prophecy of Joel: "And it shall come to pass in the last days, saith God, I will pour out my Spirit upon all flesh...and I will show wonders in heaven above, and signs in the earth beneath; blood, and fire, and vapor of smoke: the sun shall be turned into darkness, and the moon into blood, before that great and terrible day of the Lord come." But, surely, these latter "wonders" and "signs" did not transpire at the time of the indwelling of the Spirit on the day of Pentecost. For, that indwelling of the Spirit did not descend upon all flesh at that time. It was confined to the apostles and disciples, and on those believers upon whom they conferred it. That, therefore, was but an incomplete or first fulfilment of the prophecy of Joel. Hence, the true and only consistent meaning of this passage. It refers to a visible specimen of the kingdom of heaven as yet future. Accordingly, three of the Evangelists who record it, speak of it in immediate connection with the account given, that eight days after this saying, "Jesus took Peter, James, and John into a mountain apart, and was transfigured before them," together with the appearance to them of Moses and Eliajh talking with him. Here we have a complete pattern of the coming kingdom.

Christ, transfigured in His glorified humanity, together with Moses as the representative of the raised dead in Christ, and Eliajh of the living saints who shall be changed and glorified at His second appearing. And, what is decisive of this matter is, that Peter, who was one of the three, calls this very transaction "the power and coming of our Lord Jesus Christ;" that is, it was an earnest or pattern of His final coming, the "majesty" of which, he says, he was an "eye-witness of, when he was with Him on the mountain." We pass to another passage.

6. It occurs in connection with the institution of the last supper, when our Lord said, "I will no more eat thereof, until it is fulfilled in the kingdom of God;" and also, "I will not drink of the fruit of the vine, until the kingdom of God shall come." These passages, it is alleged, prove that the spiritual kingdom of God was about to be established in the time of Christ. But, surely, such expositors must have overlooked several important facts in this connection, the first of which is, the design of the institution of the Christian "passover," or last supper, as set forth by Paul, which was, that it was to be a standing memorial of Christ's passion, while personally absent from the Church. Hence, the command: "Do this in remembrance of me. For as often as ye eat this bread, and drink this cup, ye do show the Lord's death till He come." A second fact overlooked by them is this, that at the institution of the last supper, Jesus said to His disciples, "I will not drink henceforth of the fruit of the vine, until that day when I drink it new with you in my Father's kingdom." And when is that to be? The answer is, not until the twelve apostles shall be admitted to "eat and drink at Christ's table in His kingdom, and sit

on thrones judging the twelve tribes of Israel." And, more. Not until the "many" besides them shall come from the east and west, and shall sit down with Abraham, and Isaac, and Jacob, in the kingdom of heaven." I repeat: then, and not until then, will Christ celebrate His "passover" with His chosen followers. For, then "the tabernacle of God shall be with men, and He shall dwell with them, and they shall be His people." We now pass to a number of passages which are alleged to speak of the kingdom of heaven as already set up. For example, those words of Christ:

7. "If I cast out devils" (demons) "by the Spirit of God, then the kingdom of God is come unto you." All that is necessary to say by way of reply, is this: these words were spoken in the very same year in which the kingdom of God was declared to be "near," as "at hand," and "even at the doors;" and also about the time when the disciples were taught to pray, "Thy kingdom come;" which shows it to have been still future. Nor was this prayer answered by the setting up of the kingdom at any time before the crucifixion; nor after the resurrection. For, to the question of the disciples to the risen Savior, "Lord, wilt thou at this time restore the kingdom to Israel? He said unto them,"—not, mark, the kingdom never will be restored in that manner, but—"it is not for you to know the times or the seasons which the Father hath put in his own power." Clearly, therefore, this passage must be understood of that dispensation—"the kingdom of God in mystery"—which is to prepare the way for its final establishment. Another passage:

8. "The Son of Man shall send forth his angels, and they shall gather out of his kingdom all things which

offend, and which do iniquity." Therefore, this must refer to the veritable "kingdom of God, " or the Christian Church. We reply: this passage occurs in the parable of the sower and the seed. It is here to be specially born in mind, (See the 36th to the 40th verses of Matthew 13), that our Lord interprets all the parts of this parable. "The field" in which the seed, good and bad, is "sown,"

He tells us, "is the world." That is, as we have already explained, the inhabitants dwelling on the earth during the dispensation of "the kingdom of God" in "mystery." Accordingly, in this kingdom, while it lasts, "the good seed," which denotes "the children of the kingdom," and which was sown by "the Son of Man;" and "the tares," which were sown by the "enemy," i.e., the "Devil," and which denote "the children of the wicked one," "both grow together until"—when? "until the harvest," which Christ interprets to mean "the end of"—what? Now mark here... Not the end of the world of mankind, as in verse 38, but the end of the age, i.e., the age or dispensation under and during which mankind has enjoyed the advantages of a preached gospel, as in verse 40.

And now observe: The "harvest" in this parable points us to that "great day of the Lord," called "the day of judgment." But mark here, that neither in this parable, nor in that of the ten talents, or ten pounds, or of the dragnet—all of which were given to illustrate the conduct of mankind during this dispensation in accepting or rejecting the gospel offers of mercy, together with the final separation between the two classes at the time of the "harvest,"—I repeat: note that not one word is said about the resurrection and judgment of the dead. True, a resurrection will have taken place. But it will be confined to those who "have a part in the first resurrection;" those who "sleep in Christ," and with whom will be united the changed and raptured saints, who were "alive and remained unto the coming of the Lord." But this event transpires prior to the visible appearance of Christ as Judge, with His angels, "at the time of the harvest." The risen and glorified living saints,

Paul tells us, "will God bring with him" to this very "harvest." "For, know ye not," he says, "that the saints," that is, as "joint-heirs with Christ," "shall judge the world?"

The inevitable conclusion, therefore, is, that "the harvest" in this parable will consist of the judgment, not of the risen dead, but of the "quick," that is, of the living nations at the end of this age or dispensation. These will consist, first, of the converted nations, both Jewish and Gentile, who, as the saved nations in the flesh, will be admitted to that restored "dominion" (Micah 4:8) in the earth which was lost by the sin of the first Adam, now forcibly removed forever from the hand of his "serpent" seducer by, and which from then forward becomes "the kingdom of the Son of Man" under the whole heaven. The other will embrace the antichristian confederacy of the nations whom Christ will "consume by the Spirit of his mouth, and destroy with the brightness of his coming." Yes, these are they who then "know not God, and that obey not the gospel of our Lord Jesus Christ;" and "who shall be punished with everlasting destruction from the presence of the Lord, and from the glory of his power." Thus, and in no other way, will be verified the "gathering out of his kingdom of all things that offend, and that do iniquity."

There are several other passages to which we are referred,

as alleged proofs of the same view with that affirmed of the one in this parable. These are: "He that receiveth not the kingdom of God as a little child shall not enter therein." Another: "Except a man be born again, he cannot enter into the kingdom of God." And yet another, which speaks of our being "delivered from the power of darkness, and translated into the kingdom of God's dear Son." There are also a few more passages similar to these, e.g., Matthew 6:33; 11:11; 13:11, and verses 24 to 41; 52; 19:12; Luke 18:29; 1 Corinthians 6:9, 10; 15:24; Colossians 4:11; and James 2:5. In view, however, of the expositions given of the preceding passages, demonstrative of the fallacy of the popular view, that "the Church" under this dispensation and "the kingdom of God" or "of heaven" are one and the same; no further evidence is necessary to prove that the above passages are all susceptible of a similar interpretation than the following, than which it is not possible for language more clearly to set forth the distinction between the present Church state as "the kingdom of God" in "mystery," as contrasted with the future "kingdom of Christ" in manifestation. Take these two passages from Paul and Peter, both of whom, it is presumed it will be allowed, were in a state of grace. Paul says: "And the Lord shall deliver me from every evil work, and preserve me unto his heavenly kingdom." And Peter exhorts his brethren: "Wherefore the rather give diligence to make your calling and election sure; for if ye do these things, ye shall never fail: for so," he adds, "an entrance shall be administered unto you abundantly, into the everlasting kingdom of our Lord and Savior Jesus Christ."

The sum of the matter, then, is this: that Christ is the divinely constituted "Head over all things to the Church, which is his body," even that Church which had existed from the period of the first promise down to His day, and which still exists. But Christ was also born a king—"the King of the Jews." He also declared Himself to be such before the bar of Pilate. He, however, was rejected as a king, and was finally crucified by the Jews and Gentiles. Envy and malice laid Him in the sepulcher of Joseph of Arimathea. But the third day He rises again. For what purpose? Was it to set up His kingdom then? No. But, like the exiled nobleman in the parable, who, having committed his ten pounds to his servants, accompanied with the command, "Occupy till I come," "took his journey into a far country, to receive a kingdom, and to return," at which time he called them to a reckoning: so the risen Christ. Having commissioned His apostles to go to all nations, and preach the gospel to every creature, as His "witnesses," and "to take out of (or from among) the Gentiles a people for His name," He ascended, as an exiled king, to the far-off heavens, there to await, at the hand of His Father, the investiture of His royal prerogatives, when He will return with, and set up, His own rightful kingdom, and call all His servants to a reckoning for the use or abuse of the talents committed to their keeping during His prolonged absence from them.

We affirm, then,—and on this point we challenge refutation—that though Christ is identified "the Head of the Church," yet in the New Testament He is nowhere called the King of the Church. It is this circumstance, more than any other, that stamps the Roman Catholic Church with the brand of an infinitely infamous apostasy, in that her long line of pretended popes claim to be the vicegerents of Christ in His Church as temporal sovereigns! However,

I am here reminded that in Revelation 15:3, Christ is identified "the King of saints," it is no exception. In the margin it reads, King of nations. But waiving this: "King of saints" is not "king of the Church." The Jews, before New Testament times, were called "saints." No. He is their King, and as such is ordained by the oath of God "to sit on David's throne." And on this account it is that He is styled "the minister of the circumcision for the truth of God, to confirm the promises made unto the fathers."

But here arises a question, a proper answer to which is fundamental to a correct interpretation and application of that portion of the prophecies now before us. It is this: What is the position or relation of Israel and Judah to the Church of God under the Christian dispensation? An answer to this question renders it necessary to remind you:

First. That while the Messiah, Jesus, as "the minister of the circumcision for the truth of God," was the foundation, not only, but the surety and pledge given to the lineal multitudinous seed of Abraham, to "confirm the promises made to their fathers;" God the Father, as the Author and Rectoral Head of that covenant, united Himself to Israel as her husband. This is evident from the following: "The word of the Lord came to Jeremiah, saying, Go, and cry in the ears of Jerusalem, saying, Thus saith the Lord; I remember thee, the kindness of thy youth, the love of thine espousals, when thou wentest after me in the wilderness, in a land that was not sown." For, He says, "I am married unto you." But, as we have seen, when Israel turned from the Lord, and provoked the Divine jealousy by her idolatrous practices, the two names, Lo-ruhamma and Lo-Ammi (Hosea 1:6–9), were applied to her. That is, the Jehovah of Hosts as her husband, put her away, by removing her out of His sight. In other words, she was divorced from Him. The same holds true of Judah, who, on account of their "unbelief," as "the natural branches," were broken off "from the good olive-tree."

We have shown you, however, that this act of divorcement against Israel and Judah was not to be perpetual. For God, by the prophet Hosea, says: "And it shall come to pass in that day," that is, the day of their restoration, "saith the Lord, that thou shalt call me Ishi (my husband);" "and thou shalt no more call me Baali (my lord)." He says, then "will I betroth thee unto me forever: yea, I will betroth thee unto me in righteousness, and in judgment, and in loving kindness, and in mercies."

But, brethren, this is not all. "The King's Son," the Lord Jesus Christ, must have His bride also. Hence it has transpired that as the literal Israel, to whom the invitation to the marriage feast of the King's Son was first given, "all with one consent began to make excuse," and, upon being further urged, finally "refused to come;" the King-Father, in His "wrath," "said to His servants, the wedding is ready, but they which were bidden were not worthy." And then was immediately issued the command: "Go ye therefore into the highways, and as many as ye shall find, bid to the marriage." And the result was, that "the wedding was furnished with guests." Now, collateral with this, Paul's address to the unbelieving Jewish commonwealth: "Seeing ye put these things from you, and judge yourselves unworthy of everlasting life, lo, we turn to the Gentiles."

Yes. Thus the Jewish nation, for the time, was set aside. That is, she was divorced from her former relation to "the

King" as her husband. Not that the Jews were to be totally excluded from the privileges of the gospel under this dispensation. For, from the time of Paul down to the present day, they have lived in the midst of it, and, in common with the Gentile nations, it has been offered to them. So that, in their position or relation to the Church state under this economy, "Whether Jew or Greek, barbarian or Scythian, bond or free, they are all one in Christ."

But, what is to be specially noted in this connection, is, the design of this arrangement, according to that "eternal purpose which God purposed in Christ Jesus." Simeon stated this when he "declared how that God did at the first visit the Gentiles, to take out of (or from among) them, a people for His name." Now these, collectively, constitute that "holy nation, and royal priesthood, and peculiar people," who shall finally be presented unto the King-Father's "Son," as His elect or redeemed "bride," "the Lamb's wife." And the marriage nuptials shall be celebrated when the "five wise virgins," who denote her, shall hear the "midnight cry, behold the bridegroom cometh, go ye out to meet Him."

Having, therefore, in the preceding section, demonstrated, as we deferentially claim, first, the fallacy of the theory that the phrases, "the kingdom of God," "the kingdom of heaven," "the kingdom of the Son of Man," etc., are identical with the Christian Church and the millennial era; and, second, having proved that the second coming of Christ, when it does take place, will be a literally personal and *not* a spiritual coming; we now proceed to a like direct argument.

CHAPTER 2

A Premillennial Return

We now proceed by a direct scriptural argument, to demonstrate,—that the second personal coming of Christ, when it does take place, will be pre-millennial. We flatter ourself that, with those who receive the teachings of Holy Scripture as authoritative on the subject, first, of the abstract doctrine of the second personal coming of Christ; second, of the fact that that event is yet future; and, third, of the mode or form in which it is to take place; will conclude with us, that it is "not following cunningly devised fables" to tax their further indulgence, while we proceed, on the same authority, to place this matter beyond the reach of further controversy. Indeed, when we take into account the infinitely momentous interests at stake in this issue, in reference alike to the Church of God, to the nations of the earth, and to every living soul, all must unite, as with one voice, in condemnation of the thought that it is a matter of indifference, whether this august event transpires within ten, or twenty, or fifteen hundred years! We proceed, therefore, to a demonstration of this point on its abstract merits, our first argument being predicated of that notable prophecy of Daniel, chapter 2:44, 45.

"In the days of these kings, shall the God of Heaven set up a kingdom, which shall never be destroyed: and the kingdom shall not be left to other people, but it shall break in pieces and consume all these kingdoms, and it shall stand forever. Forasmuch as thou (i.e., Nebuchadnezzar) sawest that the stone was cut out of the mountain without hands, and that it break in pieces the iron, the brass, the clay, the silver, and the gold; the Great God hath made known to the king what shall come to pass hereafter: and the dream is certain, and the interpretation thereof sure."

In order to have a proper understanding of this prophecy, we must here elaborate:

1. That this vision of the colossal metallic image, taken in connection with Daniel's interpretation of it, spans the entire period called in the New Testament, "the times of the Gentiles." This period commenced with the loss to the Jewish nation of her independence under Manasseh, king of Judah, in 652 B.C., and that it ends in A.D. 1868 [or so some speculated], embracing the whole interval denoted by the mystical "seven times" Leviticus 26 and Daniel 4. With these also synchronizes the vision of Daniel's four rampant beasts, chapter 7:1–8. We observe in the next place:

2. That Daniel's interpretation of this vision teaches us to look for the final and total extermination of all earthborn monarchies, and the restoration of that theocracy under which the Jewish nation was placed prior to the period of Saul. Yes; not withstanding the enormity of their sin in casting off that government; and though they were destined, as the just punishment of their iniquity, to be

subjected to a long period of the most cruel oppressions at the hands of those earth-born monarchies whose rival national form of government to the government of God they had adopted under Saul, yet in their covenant God gives them the assurance, "For the Lord will not forsake his people for his great name's sake; because it hath pleased the Lord to make them his people." Hence, in vindicating them against the "rod" of their oppressors, He declares, that, when "the Desire of nations," i.e., the Messianic "stone," "shall come," He will "destroy" all those nations by whom, from generation to generation, they have been "scattered and peeled," reproached and oppressed. For, "Thus saith the Lord, To Jacob whom I have chosen, and Israel my servant, I will surely make a full end of all nations whither I have driven thee;...I will make Jerusalem a cup of trembling to all nations that are round about; and on that day I will make Jerusalem a burdensome stone to all nations, and they shall be cut in pieces and broken, though all the people of the earth be gathered together."

But you will ask, Why this? The answer is, because, subsequently to their renunciation of their original theocracy under Saul, who was anointed with oil out of a vial, to indicate the instability and short-lived tenure of the kingdom of Israel during his administration, God was graciously pleased to establish the perpetuity of the Israelic throne in the person of their second king, David, who was anointed with oil out of a "horn," the tenor of the covenant with whom was, that out "of the fruit of his loins, according to the flesh, God would raise up Christ to sit on his throne."

1. To return now to the prophecy under consider-

ation. The four metallic compartments of the colossal image—the gold, the silver, the brass, and the iron mingled with clay; together with the four corresponding wild beasts of Daniel—the lion, the bear, the leopard, and the nondescript monster; taken in connection with the two little horns, and the ram and he-goat of chapters 7 and 8, symbolize the four great gentile monarchies that were to bear rule in the earth during "the times of the Gentiles," i.e., the Babylonian, Medo-Persian, Grecian, and Roman: setting forth also, in reference to this last-named power (the Roman), the division of that empire into east and west, as denoted by the two iron legs of the image; and its subdivision into ten principalities, as symbolized by the ten toes of the image and the ten horns of the nondescript beast; while, on the other hand, "the little horn" of chapter 7:8 represents the papal power, and that of chapter 8:8–12 the Mohammedan impostor. In the next place:

2. The prophecy points out the destruction of these four Gentile monarchies, together with all those anti-Christian powers emanating from them, by a certain irresistible agent, called "a stone cut out of the mountain without hands." And, in the last place:

3. The period, when these four monarchies with their dependencies shall be destroyed, is explicitly signified. It is to take place "in the last days of these kings," during the last stage of their existence. The "stone" strikes the image, not on the head of gold, but on the feet of iron and clay.

As such we find, that in the Bible, as comprehending the Old and New Testaments, we are furnished with a prophetic account of the origin, the career, and final destiny of all the nations of earth, heathen, Jewish, anti-Christian, and Mohammedan, not only, but of their political and ecclesiastical constitutions, whether autocratic, despotic, monarchical, or democratic; or whether idolatrous, Papal, Mohammedan, Judaic, or Protestant.

It has been well said by the learned Bossuet and Bishop Porteus, that these above-named four monarchies "form, as it were, one vast map of Providential administration, delineated on so large a scale, and marked with such legible characters, that it cannot possibly escape our observation;" and that "this map has been held up before the eyes of all nations for the space of nearly 3,000 years, to confront the feeble objections of atheism, and to confirm the scriptural doctrine of a national Providence." However we may have overlooked this fact, in the Bible is found the most extensive and complete system of political economy of which the world can boast!

It is not our purpose, however, to enter into an application of the above prophetico-symbolic imagery denotive of the rise of these four monarchies, in detail. It must suffice to observe, that the first three of them, i.e., the Assyrio-Babylonian, Medo Persian, and Grecian, are specifically designated in Scripture, as having followed in the order of succession symbolized by the gold, silver, and brass, and by the lion, bear, and leopard, of the two visions of Nebuchadnezzar and Daniel. With the simple remark, therefore, that the term "king and kingdom" are used interchangeably to denote the same thing, I observe:

That it is evident from Daniel 1:1, that the first empire, of which Nebuchadnezzar was "king," was the Babylonian; that is, he as its sovereign, with unlimited autocratical power, was considered as representing in his person the kingdom of Babylon. The same holds true of the second, the Medo-Persian. By comparing Daniel 5:1, 2, and verses 28, 30, 31, with chapter 6:1, it will be seen that Belshazzar, the son and successor of Nebuchadnezzar, was king. Now, to this king it was that the prophet, in interpreting the mysterious handwriting on the wall of his palace, said, "God hath numbered thy kingdom, and finished it;" and, "thy kingdom is divided, and given to the Medes and Persians," (See also Daniel 8:20). So also of the third, the Grecian. "The he-goat" of Daniel 8:5, 8, 21, the prophet tells us, "is the king of Grecia, and the great horn that is between his eyes is the first king," i.e., Alexander. And, in regard to the fourth, or Roman empire, though it is not specially designated by name in either of the above visions, yet that it was that which immediately succeeded to the Grecian, is evident from the chronology of the rise and fall of the first three empires. The Babylonian existed from 612 to 538 B.C., a period of 74 years; the Medo-Persian, from 538 to 331 B.C., a period of 207 years; and the Grecian, from 331 to 168 B.C., a period of 163 years.

Now, at this last-named date, i.e., 168 B.C., the Roman empire, which was founded by Romulus 753 B.C., came to maturity, and that the last stroke in its course of conquests consisted of its subversion of Egypt, as the last of the four divisions of the empire of Alexander, as symbolized by the four-headed leopard of Daniel 7:6, and the breaking of the great horn, in the place of which there "came up four notable horns," chapter 8:8. But further evidence of this fact will appear from the following: First, that both Caesar and Augustus were titles of the Roman emperors; second, that Judea, being tributary to the prefecture of Syria when Christ was upon earth, the chief priests declared, "We have no king but Caesar;" third, that our blessed Lord himself enforced upon all the injunction, "Render therefore unto Caesar the things that are Caesar's," and finally, fourth, that the chief priests and Pharisees, apprehending the powerful influence which might accrue to Christ from the miracles wrought by Him before the people, said, "If we let Him alone, all men will believe on Him: and the Romans shall come, and take away both our place and nation." I would only add on this subject:

1. That the ten toes of the metallic image, and the ten horns of the fourth or nondescript monster, denoted the subdivision of the Roman empire into ten kingdoms, which was verified by the eruption of the Gothic and other barbarous tribes from the north into the western branch of the empire, and its final division into the various principalities of modern Europe. Nor is the matter of determining which are the ten kingdoms represented by these symbols, one of mere conjecture. The principle of territorial division—a principle adopted by Sir Isaac Newton, and sanctioned by all the most distinguished interpreters of prophecy of the present day—will be found to mark them out with almost infallible certainty.

The boundaries of the western empire at the time of which we now speak, namely, in A.D. 532, were as follows: It extended toward the west as far as Britain, which was included in it; toward the south to the Mediterranean; northward as far as the Danube and the Rhine; and eastward to the limits of the German empire. To these limits, therefore, we are to look for the ten kingdoms or subdivisions of this once mighty empire. And there, accordingly, we find them. They are as follows: 1st, Lombardy, the seat of a powerful kingdom; 2nd, Ravenna, the seat of the exarch, who reigned over a great part of Italy; 3rd, the State of Rome, the seat of the empire. To these are added, 4th, Naples, and 5th, Tuscany, forming a division of Italy into five parts. The other five kingdoms are, 6th, France; 7th, Austria; 8th, Spain; 9th, Portugal; and 10th, Great Britain.

2. Now, as there are no other ten kingdoms that can be named on this principle of a territorial division within the limits of the Roman empire, we may conclude with certainty that the above are the identical kingdoms, whose destinies are involved in the prophetic dream of Nebuchadnezzar, and the corresponding vision of Daniel. But, the "little horn" of Daniel 7:8, 20, 21, and 25, all Protestant expositors admit, symbolizes the ecclesiastical and ecclesiastico-political power of the Papacy. And:

3. The "little horn" of Daniel 8:9–25, which sprang out of one of the four notable horns of Daniel's he-goat, from the description given of him, evidently denotes a power entirely separate and distinct from the "little horn" of chapter 7:8. This will appear from the fact (without entering further into details) that the time of the appearance of the power represented by this "horn," was to be "in the latter" period of the "kingdom" of one of the "four notable horns" of Alexander's divided empire.

Whereas, the other "little horn came up among the ten horns" of Daniel's fourth or nondescript beast. Suffice it to say, that this last "little horn" arose out of the Arabian branch of Ptolemy's kingdom, that province having fallen to him by the previous conquests and union of the Arab tribes under Alexander; and, that it refers to none other than the great Mohammedan power, Yemen being the birthplace of the notorious Islam Impostor. For, though at that time it was a province of the Persian empire, yet it subsequently formed his own more distant Arab territory, from which, according to the prophet Daniel, was seen to issue those hordes of northern and northwestern Saracens—the "little horn" of Islamism—which finally "waxed exceeding great, toward the south, and toward the east, and toward the pleasant land," i.e., Palestine. Again:

4. The career of the Papal "little born" of Daniel 7:8, 20, 21, 25, was to prepare the way for the introduction upon the prophetical platform of another power, i.e., Daniel's "Willful King," chapter 11:3, 4, 35–39. The papal "little horn," though he was to have "a mouth speaking great things, chapter 7: 8, and was to "speak great words against the Most High," verse 25; yet this "willful king" is to "exalt himself, and magnify himself above every god," i.e., the true God as well as the false, and is to "speak marvelous things against the God of gods," and is to "prosper till the indignation be accomplished." Now, though the Papacy is an antichrist, yet he has never reached this excess of abomination. This "willful king," therefore, can be none other than Paul's "wicked," or "the man of sin and son of perdition," or in other words, the last antichrist, whose coming is after the working of Satan, "with all power and signs, and lying wonders, and with all deceivableness of unrighteousness in them that perish;" and "who opposeth and exalteth himself above all that is called God or that is worshiped, so that he as God sitteth in the temple of God, showing himself that he is God."

Now, if we except the " little horn " of the Papacy, Daniel 7:8, 20, 21, 25; and the "little horn" of Daniel 8:9–25, the symbol of the Turco-Ottoman power of Islamism, and which, at the last end of the indignation, " is to be broken without hand by The Prince of princes," (See Daniel 8:19, 25), and whose destruction is to immediately precede that of the others; we have in the prophecy before us, the four monarchies denoted by the four metallic components of the image which is to be smitten by "the stone cut out of the mountain without hands," "in the days of these kings."

Now, then, comes to be considered the point of principal interest in this discussion. Our text declares the total destruction of these four gigantic monarchies and their ten subdivisions, by the power of the Messianic stone, "in the days of these kings."

If, therefore, the mission of the Messianic stone, or the second coming of Christ, as we have already proved, is still future, it follows that at the time of that mission, all these four monarchies and their ten kingdoms must occupy their places on the platform of the prophetic earth. Otherwise, there is swept away the entire fabric of the prophetic word, and Christianity is left without a shield of defense against the bold and blasphemous taunt of the infidel: "Where is the promise of His coming?"

The question then is, do these four monarchies still exist? Some affirm that they do not: that they have, one and all, long since passed away, leaving nothing behind them but the historic records of their former power, magnificence, and territorial extent. Is this so? So far from it, "the sacred calendar and great almanac of prophecy" represent them as extending from the beginning of the captivity of Israel under Tiglath-Pilezer, "until the mystery of God shall be finished," when "the kingdoms of this world," by the direct agency of the Messianic stone in their complete overthrow, "shall have become the kingdom of our Lord and of His Christ."

As I would not, however, even seem to place upon the reader my unsupported assertion as authority in so important a matter, I respectfully submit the following as a solution of the difficulty in these premises.

Originally, the first of the above-named monarchies in its geographical territory, population, and government, was Babylonish. Under the second dynasty, the territory and population of Medo-Persia were annexed, and the government of the two made Medo-Persian. Under the third, in like manner, the territory and population of Greece were annexed, and the government of the three made Grecian. And, under the fourth, the territory and population were completed by the annexation of Rome, and the whole made Roman. These therefore form what, for the sake of distinction, we term the platform of the prophetical earth. Nationally and politically, this platform attained its ultimate dimensions, by the process of annexation of the one to the other successively, retaining, throughout, their national, political, and ecclesiastical characteristics—as signified by the several symbols which denote them—as so many rods in God's hand, for the chastisement of the Apostate Church, Judaic and Christian.

I repeat, therefore, that the prophetic colossal image of Nebuchadnezzar now exists in all its parts—gold, silver, brass, iron and clay; or the same, as denoted by the four corresponding beasts of Daniel—the lion, the bear, the leopard, and the nondescript beast; together with the powers denoted by the ten toes of the image and the ten horns of the fourth beast, and the two little horns of the great beast and of the rough goat. They began on the great river Euphrates, upon which stood Nineveh, the capital of Assyria, with Babylon on the Tigris. From these two cities proceeded the power which destroyed the national existence of the Ten Tribes, and brought the Two Tribes into captivity. And it is notorious, that both these ancient capitals, Nineveh and Babylon, together with the countries which they ruled, have now for eight centuries, down to the present day, been under the dominion of the Turkish or Mohammedan little horn of the rough goat.

On the other hand, the Grecian leopard, Alexander, added to the territory of the great image that very portion of Greece which, in our times, has arisen out of oppression and political death, into the state of an independent kingdom, such as it was when it first came on the prophetic stage.

And we have the Roman, still subsisting in the ten kingdoms of the west, namely, Lombardy, Ravenna, Italy, Naples, Tuscany, France, Austria, Spain, Portugal, and Great Britain.

The colossal image of Nebuchadnezzar, therefore, at this very moment, stands erect in all its parts, subjected, it is true, during the lapse of ages, to several transmutations, and undergoing various modifications, but preserving nevertheless, through all, its original metallic and beastly identity of character and of work.

Now, it is "in the days of these kings" (or kingdoms), i.e., while they still occupy their respective places and play their respective parts on the platform of the prophetic earth, that the prophet declares "the God of Heaven shall set up a kingdom, that shall stand forever." This kingdom, it would be superfluous to argue, is identical with the millennial state.

But, the setting up of this kingdom "in the days" of these "kings," is to be brought about by the mission of the Messianic Stone "cut out of the mountain without hands." This symbol, the "stone," I now observe, denotes Christ, in His official character as a Judge and a King."

With a view, however, to escape the admission which this interpretation involves, i.e., that the second coming of Jesus Christ is pre-millennial and personal, it is urged that the "stone" in the text is identical with the "mountain," and that the mountain, being symbolical of the Church, which, by her numerous agencies, is finally to evangelize the whole world; therefore, the symbolical "stone" cannot refer to Christ, but to the universally established millennial kingdom of Christ, over which He is to reign by His Spirit, till the end of a thousand years, when He is to come to raise the dead and judge the world.

This view, so generally prevalent, and sanctioned by the authority of names both of the living and of the departed which we all revere, is to be respected. I respect it. Nevertheless, I would deferentially submit, first, if the head of gold of the colossal image, and the corresponding first beast, the lion of Daniel, symbolized, personally, the Babylonian king Nebuchadnezzar, on what principle of interpretation are we to withhold the personal application of the symbolical "stone" to the King Messiah, the Lord Jesus Christ? Again, second: as Daniel, after interpreting the head of gold to signify the Babylonian king, says, "after thee shall arise another kingdom inferior to thee," thereby using the terms "king" and "kingdom" interchangeably, i.e., as denoting the same thing, how can we consistently avoid a similar use of the terms "stone" and "mountain," as symbolic of Christ and his Kingdom?

Until, therefore, our rule of interpretation of the symbolic "stone," and its application, personally, to Christ the Messiah, is proved to be unsound; we must insist, that, when the destruction of the still existing colossal image takes place, it will be effected by no less, no other agent, than the glorious personal descent of the Son of God from Heaven. Yes, by Him this colossal image, in all its parts, is to be demolished. "The stone that was cut out of the mountain without hands," is to "break to pieces the iron, the brass, the clay, the silver, and the gold." And, mark, the period in the history of these four monarchies when this destruction is to take place, is designated. It is to be in the divided state of the last or Roman dominion. The "stone," the prophet tells us, "smites the image on the feet"—the ten toes—"which were of iron and of clay." Europe, as embracing the ten horns of the nondescript beast, the present prophetical earth—Lombardy, Ravenna, the Roman State, Naples, Tuscany, France, Austria, Spain, Portugal, and Great Britain is here intended. When, therefore, the "stone" comes, "the iron, the clay, the brass, the silver, and the gold, shall be broken in pieces together, and become like the chaff of the summer threshing-floors; and the wind shall carry them away, that no place shall be found for them: and the 'stone' that smites the image shall become a great mountain, and shall fill the whole earth." Yes, then it is, that "the judgment shall sit, and they"—that is, Christ, and His co-judges and rulers, the risen saints "shall take away the dominion of the Beast, to consume and to destroy it unto the end. And the kingdom and dominion, and the greatness of the kingdom under the whole heaven, shall be given to the people of the saints of the Most High; whose kingdom is an ever lasting kingdom, and all dominions shall serve and obey Him."

CHAPTER 3

Prophecy of the Old Testament

We will next demonstrate that the ideas and language of the New Testament writers in reference to the second personal coming of Christ and the judgment of the great day, were derived from and founded upon the prophetic statements of the inspired pre-Christian Jewish writers regarding them. In illustration of this subject, we shall adopt the following passages to make our point:

Jude, verses 14, 15, "And Enoch of old, the seventh from Adam, prophesied of these, saying, Behold, the Lord cometh with ten thousand of His saints, to execute judgment upon all, and to convince all that are ungodly among them of all their ungodly deeds which they have ungodly committed, and of all their hard speeches which ungodly men have spoken against Him."

And Jude prophesied, saying—verses 20, 21: "But ye, beloved, building up yourselves on your most holy faith, praying in the Holy Ghost, keep yourselves in the love of God, looking for the mercy of our Lord Jesus Christ (i.e., at His second coming) unto eternal life."

Here it is to be observed in the outset as not a little singular, that only six out of the forty-one prophets of the Old and New Testaments, i.e., Jacob, Moses, Isaiah, David, Daniel, and Malachi, predicted of the first coming of our Lord; while most of these, together with the others, prophesied of His second personal coming.

So also, while the first class of prophets point out Christ to us in the aspect of His suffering humanity as a sin-atoning sacrifice under the law; the second class treat exclusively of His resurrected humanity, as connected with "the glory that is to follow" His sufferings, as our Triumphant King.

And now, in regard to the purposes of the second coming of Christ as presented to view in the two passages already cited, they embrace two separate and distinct parts, or acts—those of judgment and of mercy. Of judgment for the ungodly: of mercy for those who, in faith and hope, "keep themselves in the love of God, looking" for the final conferment upon them of "eternal life" at His second coming.

These two prophecies of Enoch and Jude, therefore, both relate to one and the same event, called in Scripture "the day of judgment"—"the day of the Lord"—"that great day of God Almighty," which is to take place at the time of the Second coming of Christ.

But on this, as on other momentous questions in connection with it, as we have seen, the Church of this day is unhappily at issue with herself, as to what the Scriptures teach of the nature and the order of events of "The Day of Judgment." Inasmuch, therefore, as that event hinges, so to speak, on all those numerous prophecies which foretell of the second coming of Christ in the clouds of heaven,

"In pomp and majesty ineffable," it is absolutely impossible to rightly interpret and apply them, until we shall have ascertained in what that day of judgment consists, as inclusive of both the particulars named above.

To explain. The prevailing doctrine of the Church on this subject is, that as, at the instant of the death of the righteous and the wicked, the one is immediately admitted to the perfect fruition of heavenly blessedness, and the other immediately consigned to endless consummate misery; so, there will be a universal simultaneous resurrection of both classes, that is, of the just and the unjust, by the second personal coming of Christ at the end of the millennium, as the Judge of the quick and the dead: when, having assembled all, both small and great, before His great white throne, He will open the books, try them; and, having passed sentence upon each order according to the deeds done in the body while in this life, He will say to the righteous, "Come, ye blessed of my Father, enter ye into the joys of your Lord;" and to the wicked, "Depart, ye cursed, into everlasting fire, prepared for the devil and his angels."

This theory also connects with it the additional idea, that the trial, sentences, etc., of the myriads of the raised dead, will be disposed of within the limits of a natural day of twenty-four hours, or of a very short period.

It is here also the place to remark, respecting this theory, that the millennium, at the end of which the second coming of Christ, or the day of judgment, is alleged to take place, is that state of universal peace, prosperity, and triumph of the Church on earth of a thousand years, which a body of Protestant Christians profess to look for as still future. Consequently, this theory, by placing the second coming of

Christ at the close of that period, teaches that it is post-millennial, and that we are not to look for that event until some years to come.

On the other hand, there are many in the Church—not confined to any one of, but who may be found among all the different branches of evangelical Christians in both hemispheres, and those too most eminent for their learning, piety, position—who affirm that the second personal coming of Christ is pre-millennial; also, that "the day of judgment" commences and runs parallel with the thousand years of millennial rest to the Church.

They also deny that there is to be a simultaneous resurrection both of the righteous and the wicked at the end of the millennium; but maintain that the Scriptures speak of two acts of raising the dead, the first of which takes place at the instant of Christ's second coming, at the commencement or "morning" of the millennium, according to Revelation 20:6, "Blessed and holy is he that hath part in the first resurrection, for on such the second death shall have no power; but they shall be priests of God and of Christ, and shall reign with him a thousand years." The second, at the end or evening of that period, according to Revelation 20:5, "But the rest of the dead," i.e., of the wicked dead, "lived not again until the thousand years were finished."

Hence they teach, that the "day of judgment" which takes place at the time of the second coming of Christ, instead of being limited to a natural day of twenty-four hours, opens with an act of mercy to the righteous, both dead and living, according to the statement of Paul, 1 Thessalonians 4:13–17: "But I would not have you ignorant, brethren, concerning them which are asleep, that ye sorrow not, even as them which have no hope," i.e., the wicked dead; "for, if we believe that Jesus died and rose again, even so them also which sleep in Jesus will God bring with Him. For this we say unto you by the word of the Lord, that we which are alive and remain unto the coming of the Lord, shall not prevent them which are asleep," i.e., from being raised: "for the Lord himself shall descend from heaven with a shout, with the voice of the archangel, and with the trump of God: and the dead in Christ shall rise first." Nor this only: for the apostle adds: "Then," i.e., at the time of the second coming of Christ, "we which are alive and remain, shall be caught up together with them," i.e., the raised dead in Christ, "in the clouds, to meet the Lord in the air; and so shall we ever be with the Lord."

But, this "great day of God Almighty" also opens with an act of judgment upon the wicked, who shall then be alive upon the earth. We again quote from Paul, 2 Thessalonians 1:7–10: "And to you who are troubled rest with us, when the Lord Jesus shall be revealed from heaven with His mighty angels in flaming fire, taking vengeance on them that know not God, and that obey not the gospel of our Lord Jesus Christ; who shall be punished with everlasting destruction from the presence of the Lord, and from the glory of his power: when He shall come to be glorified in His saints, and to be admired in all them that believe...in that day," i. e., the day of their first resurrection, as above described.

This act of judgment, therefore, takes effect, not upon the wicked dead, but upon the living nations who, "in that day," "know not God and obey not the gospel of Christ." It will fall upon all those who are then found within the pale of the apostate Christian Church, and of the last great Democratico-Atheistic Confederacy against Christ and His saints, who, being "consumed"—as Paul (2 Thessalonians 2:8) says it will be "with the spirit of the mouth, and destroyed by the brightness of the coming" of the Lord Jesus; and, thus numbered with the dead, they "shall not live again," i.e., be raised from the dead, "until" at the close of the same second coming of Christ, when He shall appear "seated upon His great white throne," to execute upon them the final act of judgment, by causing all of them, "both small and great," gathered from the "sea," and "death" or the grave, "to stand before God" when "the thousand years are finished." (See Revelation 20:5).

Consequently, this latter class of prophetical interpreters affirm of this "day of judgment," inasmuch as it comprehends the twofold acts of rewards and of punishments, that it spans the whole period of the thousand years of millennial blessedness. This is founded on what they claim that the Scriptures teach in regard to the official character and functions of the risen and glorified saints, to wit, that being "a chosen generation, a royal priesthood, an holy nation and a peculiar people;" as the "heirs of God and joint-heirs with Christ," they are constituted "kings and priests unto God and his Father;" and that, as such, they will wear "crowns," "sit on thrones with Christ," and that "judgment shall be given unto them," to "judge the twelve tribes of Israel," and also to "rule the nations with a rod of iron."

Thus they "shall live and reign with Christ a thousand years on the earth and over the saved nations, Jewish and Gentile, in their millennial state. The prophet Isaiah, speaking of Messiah in direct reference to this period as "the Branch that was to grow out of the root of Jesse," says, "With righteousness shall He judge the poor, and reprove with equity for the meek of the earth." And to this he adds, "and He shall smite the earth"—the four Gentile monarchies—"with the rod of His mouth, and with the breath of His lips shall he slay the wicked."

Here then, we submit, we have a clearly defined double act of mercy and judgment, such as is to characterize the entire millennial period of the Church as that "great day of the Lord" called "the day of judgment," of which the Scriptures speak. And, at the close of this day, when the wicked dead are raised, tried, and condemned, "Death," i.e., he that "had the power of death, which is the Devil;" and hell (Hades), where the spirits of the wicked dead, prior to the resurrection of their bodies, had been "reserved for chains under darkness against the day of judgment and perdition of ungodly men;" together with all who are not then "found written in the book of life," shall be "cast into the lake of fire," which is "the second death."

This latter exposition of the nature and order of events of "the day of judgment," we shall now proceed to demonstrate, furnishes the only method by which to harmonize that large portion of the prophecies of the Old and New Testaments, which relate to the second personal coming of Christ. In doing this, we shall show, in support of the thesis which forms the subject of this chapter, that the ideas and language of the New Testament writers regarding it, were all derived from and founded upon the prophetic statements of it, as made by the inspired pre-Christian Jewish writers. In other words, it will be seen that the doctrine of a future judgment, with its antecedents, accompaniments, and consequents, as taught by our blessed Lord, and by the apostles Peter, Paul, and John, in the Epistles and the Apocalypse, all synchronize throughout with that of the Book of Daniel. We will begin with the following comparison:

When the prophetical times of Daniel are fully expired, the Son of Man comes in the clouds of heaven to the Ancient of Days, and having smitten the metallic colossal image on the feet of iron and clay, and destroyed the Papal and last anti-christian powers, there is "given unto Him dominion, and glory, and a kingdom, that all people, and nations, and languages should serve him," (Daniel 2:34, 35, 44; 7:11–14).

When Luke's "times of the Gentiles" are fulfilled, the "signs in the sun, moon, and stars, together with distress of nations, men's hearts failing them for fear and for looking after those things that are coming on the earth;" then shall the budding of the fig-tree give warning of "the coming of the Son of Man in a cloud with power and great glory," to indicate that "the kingdom of heaven is nigh at hand," and that the time is come for the redemption of Israel. Compare Luke 21:24, 25, 27, 28, with Romans 11:25, 26.

The whole period of "the times of the Gentiles" runs contemporary with the prophetical "seven times," or 2520 years of Israel's chastisement, Leviticus 26:18, 21, 24, 28, at the close of which, Daniel's 1335 days or years run out (Daniel 11:12), when the angel declares to him, that "God will accomplish to scatter the power of his holy people," i.e., the Jews (Daniel 12:7).

This latter period of Daniel, is the same with Paul's

"fullness of the Gentiles," Romans 11:25; see also Luke 21:24; which being "come in," i.e., ended, he tells us that "the Deliverer shall come to Zion, and shall turn away ungodliness from Jacob," and so, "all Israel shall be saved." (Romans 11:26).

We shall now proceed to show, that as the first coming of Christ was to be while the fourth or Roman kingdom— symbolized by the two iron legs of the image, Daniel 2:33, and the nondescript monster of chapter 7—was yet in being; so the second is to take place when it shall end.

On this subject, the profoundly learned Joseph Mede (1586–1639) says:

> The mother text of Scripture, with which the Church of the Jews grounded the name and expectation of the great day of judgment, with the circumstances belonging to it, and where upon almost all the descriptions and expositions in the New Testament have reference, is that vision of the 7th chapter of Daniel of a session of judgment when the fourth beast came to be destroyed: where this great court is represented after the manner of the great Sanhedrin, or consistory of Israel; where upon they sat upon seats placed semi-circular before them. "I beheld," said Daniel, (chapter 7:9, 10), "till the thrones were pitched down," (namely, for the senators to sit upon), "and the Ancient of Days did sit. I beheld, till the judgment was set" (that is, the whole San-

hedrin), "and the books were opened."

Here we see both the form of judgment delineated, and the name of judgment expressed; which is afterward twice more repeated; first, in the amplification of the tyranny of the wicked horn (verses 20, 21), the symbol of the Papacy, which (it is said) continued "till the Ancient of Days came, and judgment was given to the saints of the Most High:" and the second time, in the angel's interpretation, (verse 26), "But the judgment shall sit, and they shall take away his dominion, to consume and to destroy it unto the end." Where, we observe also that cases of dominion of blasphemy, and apostasy, and the like, belonged to the jurisdiction of the great Sanhedrin.

From this description it came that the Jews gave it the name of the day of judgment and the day of the great judgment: where upon, in the Epistle of Jude (verse 6), it is called "The judgment of the great day."

From the same description they learned that the destruction then to be should be by fire; because it is said (verse 9), "His throne was like a fiery flame, and his wheels as burning fire;" (and verse 11), "The beast was slain, and his body destroyed, and given to the burning flame."

From the same foundation are derived those expressions in the gospel, where this day is intimated or described: "The Son of Man shall come in the clouds of heaven"—"the Son of Man shall come in the glory of the Father, with his holy angels:" forasmuch as it is said here, "Thousand thousands ministered unto him;" and that Daniel saw "One like unto the Son of Man coming with the clouds of heaven, and He came unto the Ancient of Days, and they brought Him near before Him."

Hence Paul learned that "the saints should judge the world" (1 Corinthians 6:2); because it is said that "many thrones were set;" and (verse 22), by way of explanation, that "judgment was given to the saints of the Most High."

Hence the same apostle learned to overcome the false fears of the Thessalonians, that the day of Christ's second coming was near at hand; because that day could not be, till the man of sin were first come, and should have reigned an appointed time. (2 Thessalonians 2:3); forasmuch as Daniel had foretold that it should be so, and that his destruction should be at the appearing of the Son of Man in the clouds; whose appearing, therefore, should not be till then. Paul says, "whom the Lord shall destroy at his coming." Daniel's wicked horn is Paul's man of sin [rather, we should say, the forerunner], as the Church from her infancy interpreted it.

But, to go on. While this judgment sits, and when it had destroyed the fourth beast by the coming of the Son of Man in the clouds of heaven, He receives "dominion, and glory, and a kingdom, that all people, nations, and languages should serve and obey him." (verse 14); which kingdom is explained three times afterwards to be the millennial kingdom of "the saints of the Most High." (verses 18, 22, 27).

These grounds being laid, Mede proceeds. I argue as follows: The kingdom of the Son of Man and of the saints of the Most High in Daniel's vision, begins when the great judgment sits.

The kingdom in the Apocalypse, wherein the saints reign with Christ a thousand years (Revelation 20:4, 6), is the same with the kingdom of the Son of Man and of the saints of the Most High in the vision of Daniel.

Therefore, it also begins at the great judgment. That the kingdom in Daniel and that of a thousand years in the Apocalypse are one and the same kingdom, appears as follows: First, because they begin at the destruction of the fourth beast: that in Daniel, when the beast (then ruling in the eleventh little wicked horn) is slain, and his body destroyed, and given to the burning flame (Daniel 8:11, 22, 27): that in the Apocalypse, when "the beast" (i.e., the two-horned beast from the earth, having a mouth like the Dragon), "and the false prophet" (i.e., the Papal wicked horn in Daniel), "were taken, and both cast alive into a lake burning with fire and brimstone." (Revelation 19:20, 21).

Secondly, because John begins the kingdom of a thousand years from the same session of judgment described in Daniel, as appears by his parallel expression borrowed from it:

Daniel says, chapter 7:9: "I beheld, till the thrones were pitched down...and the judgment sat." "And judgment was given to the saints of the Most High." "And the saints possessed the kingdom:" i.e., with the Son of Man who came in the clouds.

John says, chapter 20:4: "I saw thrones, and they (i.e., the risen and raptured saints), sat upon them." "And the saints lived and reigned with Christ a thousand years." "To him that overcometh, will I grant to sit with me in my throne." (Revelation 3:21). "And I will give them power over the nations." (Revelation 2:26).

Now, if this be sufficiently proved, that the thousand years begin with the day of judgment, it will appear further out of the Apocalypse, that the judgment is not consummated until they are ended: for Gog and Magog's destruction, and the universal resurrection of the wicked dead, together with the final destruction which is to change and purify the globe, will not be until then: therefore, the whole thousand years is included in the day of judgment.

Therefore, it will follow, that whatever Scripture speaks of a kingdom of Christ to be at His second appearing, or at the destruction of [the last] antichrist, it must be the same which Daniel saw would be at that time—and so, consequently, the kingdom of a thousand years, which the Apocalypse includes between the beginning and consummation of the great judgment.

Finally, to sum up the whole in a few words. The day of Christ's second coming, and the great day of judgment which opens it, commence at the close of the 1335 days or years of Daniel 12:12, when the vengeance of God begins to be poured out upon the little Papal horn; is continued upon the last anti-christian or atheistic confederacy, headed by the two-horned Apocalyptic beast from the earth (Revelation 13:11–17), or Paul's "man of sin and son of perdition" (2 Thessalonians 2:3); extends through the period of the millennium and terminates with the final destination of all mankind, by the reward of the redeemed in their admission to that "inheritance which is incorruptible," in the "new earth and heavens" which "God will create;" and by the punishment of the wicked in Gehenna fire of everlasting torments.

It consequently follows, that this second coming of Christ comprehends not two separate and distinct comings, but two manifestations of one and the same event: the one at the commencement of the millennial period, to raise the sleeping dead in Christ, and change and glorify the living saints, and to destroy the last antichrist and his God-denying confederacy; and the other, at the close of it, to punish the Gog and Magog hosts that compass the camp of the saints and the beloved city, by fire from heaven; to raise the wicked dead, both small and great, from their graves, and the sea and Hades; and, arraigning them before the Judge, who now appears, for the first, seated on His great white throne, to try them according to the deeds done in the body, and to consign them, together with death and Hades, to the perdition of ungodly angels and men.

At this point, therefore, time closes, and eternity begins. Of this Paul spoke when he said: "Then cometh the end, when He (i.e., Christ) shall have delivered up the kingdom (millennial) to God, even the Father, when He shall have put down all rule, and all authority and power;" for, "He must reign, until He hath put all enemies under His feet; the last of these enemies is "Death," so, "when all things shall be subdued unto Him, then shall the Son also himself be subject unto Him that put all things under Him, that God may be all in all."

Thus much, then, in regard to the opposite views prevalent in the Church of this day, as to what constitutes the scriptural doctrine of the second coming of Christ and of the future judgment.

But we now deferentially submit, that we have pointed out the fallacy of the various theories:

I. That all that the prophetic Scriptures teach on this subject, were verified by the return of the Jews from the Babylonish captivity.

II. That they were verified by the events which

preceded, accomplished, and followed the invasion and destruction of Jerusalem, by the Roman army, in A.D. 70.

III. That they received their accomplishment by the overthrow of paganism and the establishment of Christianity in the Roman empire under Constantine the Great at and after A.D. 323.

IV. Of those who allege, that the kingdom and reign of Christ on earth at His second coming will be spiritual; and that "the times of the Gentiles" are identical with the establishment of the Christian Church, the dispensation of which is to continue until the close of the millennial age.

V. In addition to the inferences derivable from our scriptural arguments and historical and philosophical facts against the second personal coming of Christ as being post-millennial; what we have advanced by way of a direct argument, as demonstrative that, when that event does take place, it will be pre-millennial. We have adduced the scriptural proof, that the ideas and language of the New Testament writers in reference to the second personal coming of Christ and the judgment of the great day as future, were all derived from and founded upon the prophetical statement of the inspired pre-Christian Jewish writers regarding them. This last-named circumstance of itself, unless it can be shown to be fallacious, settles forever the question as to the foundation of the synchronisms of the Gospels, Epistles, and the Apocalypse, with the Book of Daniel, in regard to this great fundamental doctrine of the judgment-coming of the Lord; and it cannot fail to appeal, with a corresponding force and power, to the heart and conscience of every lover of the truth as it is in Christ.

It may, however, be of service here to present the

divergence between the prevailing theory and its opposite, in juxtaposition. It is maintained by the Church at large:

1. That the second personal coming of Christ is post-millennial, and that the day of judgment does not commence until the close of that period

2. That all the dead, both righteous and wicked, are then to be simultaneously raised, and being tried, are justified or condemned, the righteous being taken to heaven, and the wicked consigned to hell. And,

3. That the day of judgment is limited to the short period of a natural day of twenty-four hours.

By us, it is believed:

1. That the second personal coming of Christ is pre-millennial, and that the day of judgment commences at the opening of that period.

2. That then "the dead in Christ are raised first, and the living saints changed and glorified; while "the rest of the dead" (i.e., the wicked dead) are not raised "until the thousand years are ended" (Revelation 20:8).

3. That the day of judgment runs contemporary with the whole period of the millennium of a thousand years.

In conclusion, then, we observe, first that it is clear that these conflicting views, so absolutely opposite, cannot both be according to "the mind of the Spirit," as revealed in Holy Scripture. Nor can it be pretended on any legitimate principles of scriptural interpretation, that the voice of the many against the comparatively few, is any evidence of the truth of the popular theory on this subject. To admit this, would be to reverse the order of evidence in proof of any doctrine of Holy Scripture. "The voice of the people is the voice of God" is not the criterion by which to decide the question, "what is truth?" It was the voice of the people, both Jews and Gentiles, that crucified God's dear Son while, except the weeping Mary, and a few others who clung around the cross to the last, even the few timid disciples who had followed Jesus during his ministry, "stood afar off!" Indeed, all history shows, that the true faith of the Church, doctrinally, has always been found, not with the many, but with the few. It was so at the time of the flood. It was so in the time of Abraham. It was so in the time of the prophet Elijah. It was so at the time of the first coming of our blessed Lord, and also during His ministry and that of His apostles. And Christ himself declared prophetically, that so it shall be immediately before and at the time of His second appearing: "As it was in the days of Noah," even so shall it be in the days of the Son of Man." And to this Paul prophetically adds that "that day shall not come, except there come a falling away first." While Peter, speaking prophetically of the same event, declares, that "in the last day shall scoffers arise, walking after their own lusts, and saying, Where is the promise of His coming? For since the fathers have fallen asleep, all things continue as they were from the beginning of the creation." Does it not then behoove us to beware, lest we at this day should be found among the "scoffers" of these "last times?"

And, second, we may see from this subject the error, the palpable injustice of confounding, as many do, the millenarian system of interpreting the prophetic Scriptures—which is that substantially advocated by us—with that of Millerism. The truth of the matter is, that Millerism differs in nothing from the popular theory respecting the day of judgment as future, except in the single article of anticipating the time of Christ's second coming. Both affirm that Christ is to come at the close of "the times of the Gentiles," with this difference: according to the popularly received views, that event is not to transpire for some 1,500 years or more; whereas the Father of Millerism, alleging that the times of the Gentiles "closed in A.D. 1843, as terminating the 6,000 years from the creation and fall, affirmed that Christ would come then, simultaneously raise the dead, both just and unjust, save the righteous, destroy the wicked, and wrap the globe in the flames of the last universal destruction; having done which, mankind were to enter upon their eternal state of bliss or of woe.

On the other hand, millenarianism maintains that "the times of the Gentiles," and the millennial period of the Church, are two separate and distinct dispensations, and also, that while Christ's second coming is pre-millennial, the universal destruction is post-millennial. And therefore, that time does not close, and eternity begin, at the termination of the "times of the Gentiles;" but that it continues to run on to the end of the peace, prosperity, universal righteousness and glory to man, of the mild and gracious reign of "The Prince of Peace."

The way is now prepared, for the discussion of the only remaining topic directly connected with "the great theological question" in reference to the Second Coming of Christ, as indicated by the following chapter.

CHAPTER 4

Nature of the Resurrected State

Having, in the preceding pages, agreeably to my original design, discussed at considerable length the various theories which relate to the second coming of Christ, whether it is to be pre- or post-millennial; the subject of the mode or manner of that coming calls for additional remark. The question regarding it involves a more extended inquiry into the nature of the resurrection, in its application to our blessed Lord and Savior Jesus Christ, and to the dead, both just and unjust.

The question is, does it consist of a purely spiritual, or of a literal or corporeal resurrection? On this subject we premise, that, whatever was the mode or form of the resurrection of our Lord, that mode or form will characterize the resurrection of "all that are in their graves" generally; and in respect to the saints in particular, there will be an exact correspondence between it and the resurrected state of Christ, in accordance with the explicit declaration of the Apostle John, 1st Epistle, chapter 3:2, "Beloved, now are we the sons of God, and it doth not yet appear what we shall be, but we know that when He shall appear, we shall be like Him, for we shall see Him as He is." But, the popularly received theory of the Church of this day is, that the righteous, at the instant of death, enter upon a state of perfect and consummate blessedness of God in heaven, and of the wicked in hell, and that their resurrection will consist of their being changed into a purely spiritual state.

It follows, therefore, on the principle of homogeneity, that the resurrection of Christ, in its mode or form, was of a purely spiritual nature. For, to argue that the resurrection of Christ was a literal or corporeal resurrection, while that of the saints is purely spiritual, is totally irreconcilable with, and ignores the above statement of John. But, this popular theory of a purely spiritual resurrection, we maintain, tends to cut up, root and branch, what we affirm to be the scriptural doctrine of a literal or corporeal resurrection of the dead, whether in respect either of Christ, or of the just and unjust.

It is necessarily founded upon the hypothesis, that "the soul only is the man," that is, the person. But in direct opposition to this theory—which we hold to be of the species of ancient Sadduceism—we maintain, that the soul, plus the body, is the man, that is, the person. In other words, we mean, that man, at his creation, was constituted a complex being, consisting of body and soul; and therefore that, in order to preserve the personality of man in its integrity after death, the body must be literally raised from the dead, and reunited to the soul; and also, that such a resurrection is common to both Christ and the saints, together with "the rest of the dead" spoken of in Revelation 20:5.

By the term spiritual, I mean that which is not perceivable to the senses, immaterial, incorporeal, invisible. To illustrate its nature and operations, our blessed Lord employs the following striking metaphor: "The wind bloweth where it listeth, and thou hearest the sound thereof, but canst not tell whence it cometh, and whither it goeth; so is every one that is born of the spirit. Here, that material element, the "wind" or air in motion, from its most powerful but subtle and invisible properties, is used to denote the nature of the infinite and eternal godhead, whose existence, however attested by the magnitude and grandeur of creation's work, or by the fruits of man's regenerated being, is nevertheless, in His divine essence, hidden from mortal eye, "The blessed and only Potentate, the King of kings, and Lord of lords, who only hath immortality, dwelling in light, which no man can approach unto; whom no man hath seen, nor can see." Therefore the word spirit—in Hebrew *ruach*, in Greek *pneuma*, and in Latin *spiritus*—as significant of the divine essence, is applied, first, to the Father, —"God is a spirit"—and of whom Jesus declared, "No man hath seen God at any time." And second, to the Third Person of the adorable Trinity, who, proceeding from the Father and the Son, energized the chaotic elements of the material world, bringing order out of confusion; and in the moral world, inspires, illumines, regenerates, and sanctifies the redeemed, I only add on this subject, that our Lord, by way of contrasting His complex nature with that of a Being purely spiritual, says to the eleven disciples among whom He appeared in His resurrected body, "Why are ye troubled and why do thoughts arise in your hearts? Behold my hands and my feet; it is I myself. Handle me, and see: for a spirit hath not flesh and bones, as ye see me have."

This brings me to a definition of the word. This word means, that which is opposed to spiritual or immaterial, as, a material or corporeal body. Such a material existence, however, is not to be understood as excluding from it all connection with what is spiritual. They may coexist with each other. In man, they do so coexist. Hence the term *pneuma* is applied to the human soul or spirit, breathed into the newly-created corporeal form of man by God himself, expressly to distinguish it on the one hand from his body, *soma*; and on the other from his soul, *psyche*. Man, indeed, is constituted of three parts, body, soul, and spirit; the latter, the spirit, consisting of the animal life, as forming the connecting link between the body and the soul, and which, though composed of matter, yet being refined and attenuated to its utmost capacity, like heat which is material—is invisible and intangible, a refined, active substance, subject to the laws of matter, and, though differing from every other modification of it, yet is equally liable to decomposition. This is in exact harmony with the philosophy of the inspired Paul on this subject, 1 Thessalonians 5:23, where he says, "I pray God your whole spirit and soul and body be preserved blameless unto the coming of our Lord Jesus Christ."

From the very intimate but yet inscrutable affinities subsisting between the soul and spirit, however, man for the most part has come to be regarded simply as constituted of body and soul, or the corporeal and the spiritual: the body, the vehicle of the soul's manifestations; the body, originally created immortal, yet, on account of sin, subject to death; the soul, immaterial, indestructible.

Such, then, is man. And such a man—I would utter

the sentiment with the deepest solemnity—such a man, sin excepted, was our blessed Lord and Savior, Jesus Christ. Yes. "According to the eternal purpose" of self-manifestation, which the spiritual "invisible God" the Father "purposed in Christ Jesus our Lord," "a body," corporeal, visible, was "prepared" for Him; and, "in the fullness of the time," was assumed by Him of the Virgin Mary, by "the power of the Holy Ghost." Of that "body," that of the newly-created Adam was "the figure." Nor of the body only. For, as "God breathed" into the "nostrils" of "the first man who" "was of the earth, earthy," and he thereby "became a living soul;" so we read of the Lord Jesus, that "His soul was exceeding sorrowful." Nor does the corresponding relation between "the first man" as the figure or type of "the second Adam, the Lord from heaven" as the anti-type, end here. Did the first Adam die? So did the second. The following Pauline statements illustrate and confirm these points: "He (Christ) took not on Him the nature of angels, but He took on Him the seed of Abraham. Wherefore it behooved Him, in all things, to be made like unto His brethren." "For as much, then, as the children are partakers of flesh and blood, He also himself likewise took part of the same; that, through death, He might destroy him that had the power of death, that is, the Devil; and deliver them who, through fear of death, were all their lifetime subject to bondage."

With this distinction, therefore, between the nature of the purely spiritual, and that which is corporeal, kept in view, I now remark, that, whenever the Scriptures speak of the first and the third persons of the adorable Trinity, namely, the Father and the Holy Ghost, whatever their acts and operations, either in the world of nature or of grace, they are always presented to the mind in their incorporeal, indivisible, and infinitely spiritual essence. That is, that they are not cognizable to the senses.

It remains to be seen whether the same holds true of what the Scriptures affirm of the second person of the Trinity, the Lord Jesus Christ, as the manifested God-Man Mediator. The whole question, therefore, philosophically considered, turns upon the single point as to what constitutes personality.

On the principle that the soul plus the body is the man, then, the soul cannot say to the body, "I have no need of thee;" nor can the body say to the soul, "I have no need of thee." This reciprocity of dependence each upon the other, as arising from the joint connection of the two, constitutes essential personality. And, as the person consists of soul and body conjointly, so, personal identity, taken in connection with the scriptural doctrine of the resurrection, is dependent on two circumstances: the first, the perpetuity of the material body in its connection with the soul during life; and the second, the resurrection of the same body, and its reunion with the soul after death.

Now, in reference to the first of these conditions, i.e., the perpetuity of the material body during life, it is provided for by a law of nature adapted by the Creator to that end. "Life is maintained by continued combustion. The oxygen of the air we breathe combines with the food we eat. Carbonic acid is given out by the breath and the pores of the skin. Fresh carbon is required to maintain the supply, and to compensate for the waste produced. The sensation of hunger urges us to eat, and thus fresh fuel is added to the fire. Every time we breathe we inhale oxygen. Every time we eat we swallow carbon. By this simple process, life is maintained." And, whatever changes may occur in the physical constitution of man, as produced by these chemical combinations from infancy to old age, the supply, as seen in the gradual growth of the body, exceeding the waste, his material nature is sustained in its entire integrity. At death, "the oxygen is inspired for the last time, and the combustion which maintains life, of course, ceases. The fire is put out, to be rekindled once for all [and, so far as the dead in Christ are concerned, after a heavenly manner] at the resurrection." As to the allegation that, under the above-named law for the maintenance of animal life, the body undergoes an entire change every seven, or as some say, every three years, so that we have not the same body now that we had three, or seven, or ten years ago; a scar, contracted in childhood, and retained to old age, is a sufficient refutation.

And, what is true of the "children" as "partakers of flesh and blood," is equally true of that adorable Redeemer, who took upon Him their nature. Of the child Jesus, we read, that He "grew, and increased in stature."

The second condition of personal identity, I said, consisted in the resurrection of the same body, and its reunion with the soul, after death. Now, observe. By the phrase, the resurrection of the same body, I mean, not that it (i.e., the body of the believer) will be the same as to its corporeal condition, both before and after the resurrection; for we read that "we shall all be changed, at the last trump." This "vile body shall be made like unto Christ's glorious body." By the phrase, the same body, then, I mean the identity of the pre-resurrection body with the post-resurrection body, when it shall be reunited to the soul.

Personality, then, as we have seen—understanding the soul as including that of the spirit—consists of two parts, body and soul. At death, these two parts are dissociated from each other. The body is laid in the grave. The soul is in Hades, the place of the departed, whether of happiness or misery. The body, taken separately, though not ourself, is a part of ourself, and it is that part which dies. But, the soul never dies. Nothing is more irrational and absurd, therefore, than to talk of the resurrection of the soul. True, the soul, if saved, must also be changed in its moral character, and this change in Scripture is called both a new creation and a resurrection. But, this new creation and resurrection of the soul must take place in this life. It follows, that, in order to complete our personality, the same body that is laid in the grave, subject to such a change as is necessary to fit it to that end, must be raised, and reunited to the soul.

The apostle Paul, in answer to the question, "How are the dead raised up and with what body do they come?" answered: "Thou fool, that which thou sowest is not quickened, except it die: and that which thou sowest, thou sowest not that body that shall be, but bare grain." Here we are plainly taught, that the seed which dies, is the seed that is brought to life. This representation accords with fact, and is sanctioned by common consent. The difference of the raised body, i.e., "that body that shall be," from the body as dead, is illustrated by the difference between the seed sown, and the plant which springs from it. The plant, the raised body, has a pericarp [capsule], whereas the seed sown has none, but is a "naked seed." It has been objected to the personal identity of the dead with the raised body, as drawn from Paul's analogy between the seed sown and made alive, that insect transformation, e.g., that of the butterfly, is against it. But, let us see. The following comparison, if I am not mistaken, will show that there is a perfect analogy between them. On close examination, each will be found to pass through the four following stages. Thus: The Insect. (butterfly), 1. The egg. 2. The larva, or caterpillar. 3. The pupa, or chrysalis. 4. The imago, or perfect insect. Man: 1. Man, in embryo. 2. At birth—a crawling worm. 3. At death, his pupa, or chrysalis state. 4. At the resurrection, his imago, or perfect state, when he comes forth clothed with an immortal body.

The fallacy of the above objection consists in its making the soul to pass at once from the second, the larva, or caterpillar state, to that of the fourth, or the imago or perfect state; thus overlooking the important fact that the third, the pupa or chrysalis state, is intermediate between the two. Nothing therefore is more evident than the perfect analogy which exists between the insect and the human transformations; for, "The butterfly, the representative of the soul, is prepared in the larva for its future state of glory; and if not destroyed by the ichneumons and other enemies to which it is exposed, symbolical of the vices that seek to destroy the spiritual life of the soul, it will come to its state of repose in the pupa, which is its Hades; and at length, when it assumes the imago, break forth with new powers and beauty to final glory, and the reign of love." I pass to another argument.

The resurrection of "dead persons" is an elemental doctrine. Thus Paul, Hebrews 6:1, 2, makes "the resurrection of the dead" one of the first "principles of the doctrine of

Christ." And no marvel. For Jesus himself had declared, "The hour is coming, in which all that are in their graves shall come forth."

Now, whether we understand the expression, a dead person, to denote a dead body; or the soul of a dead person; or the soul and body conjointly; the Scriptures will be found to treat the subject under all these aspects, to show that the resurrection from the dead consists of a revival to life, by a reunion of soul and body.

Take the first sense—where a dead person is understood in the sense of a dead body. One who had died was carried out, "the only son of his mother." "Dead persons are raised." "Women received their dead raised to life again." In these and numerous other passages, a dead person means a dead body raised to life.

Take the second sense—where the soul is used to denote a dead person. "I saw under the altar the souls of them that were slain for the word of God, and for the testimony which they held," i.e., the martyrs of Jesus.

Take the third sense—where a dead person is understood of the soul and body conjointly. Such are all those passages which speak of "a resurrection of (or from among) dead persons." Thus, "the dead in Christ shall rise first." Here, as predicated of the resurrection, the meaning is, that those who shall share in the blessedness of "the first resurrection," are raised by a reunion of soul and body, the former being redeemed from Hades, the latter, from the grave. This reunion, therefore, both of body and soul, is essential to the integrity of the entire person.

But, I pass to a third argument. It is this: This identity of the dead body with the raised body, is proved from those passages in which the "person" is expressed, and "the body" is intended. Man, after death, does not cease to exist. True, a change has taken place in the mode of that existence. The soul and body are separated. But to say, on this account, that the soul and spirit alone constitute man in the whole integrity of his complex nature, is as contrary to sound philosophy as it is repugnant to Scripture.

The Mosaic account of man's creation is decisive of this. "The Lord God formed man of the dust of the ground; and breathed into his nostrils the breath of life, and man became a living soul." Here is man in the integrity of his nature as constituted of body and soul while living. There must, therefore, in order to retain that integrity in man's resurrected state, be a complete parallelism. Otherwise, man loses his personal identity. Paul's argument of analogy in the fifteenth chapter of 1 Corinthians, between the dead seed sown and made alive, and the dead body buried and raised, proves this parallelism. I have said that the soul, when separated from the body at death, still lives in a state of perfect consciousness in Hades. On the other hand, the popular idea regarding the state of the dead body when laid in the grave is that life is totally extinct. And yet, death, in Scripture, is represented figuratively as a state of sleep. Speaking of the dead in general, Daniel says of them "the sleepers in the dust of the earth." So the martyr Stephen is said to "have fallen asleep." And Christ said of Lazarus, "Our friend Lazarus sleepeth." All that I would suggest as intended by these and similar passages, is, that they illustrate the minuteness of the analogy between the seed sown and the buried body. The seed contains within itself a vital principle, which, when sown, lies in a dormant state, and this state the apostle calls death. Can the apostle, then, mean anything less, anything else, than that the dead bodies of those who "sleep in the dust of the earth" are also possessed of a principle of vitality? Is the latter case less possible with God than the former? Paul thought not. But, recognizing the identity of the dead with the living body, he says, "and I pray God your whole spirit and soul and body be preserved, blameless, unto the coming of our Lord Jesus Christ."

The above facts I have adduced simply to show why it is that the Scriptures, when speaking of the dead, make mention of "the person," when "the body" only is intended. I give the following illustration: In the twenty-third chapter of Genesis, the phrase, burying the dead, occurs seven times; and at the close of it we read, "Abraham buried Sarah his wife." Again. "Isaac died...and his sons Esau and Jacob buried him." "Miriam died, and was buried." "Aaron died, and was buried." "God buried Moses in a valley in the land of Moab." "David was buried in the city of David." And, coming to the New Testament, we read of Tabitha or Dorcas who had died, that when Peter entered the chamber where the corpse was laid, "turning him to the body, he said, Tabitha, arise!" In the account of the death of Lazarus (John, chapter 11), the expressions, "He had lain in the grave four days already" (verse 17); "Where have ye laid him?" (verse 34); "They took away the stone, where the dead man was laid," (verse 41), all go to show that the evangelist, in speaking of the dead body of Lazarus, spoke of him personally.

And this mode of speech, is in perfect harmony with that in common use on this subject. Thus we say: "Washington lies buried in the family vault at Mount Vernon." "Pitt and Fox lie side by side in Westminster Abbey."

But, in addition to the above fact, there is yet one other which I must not pass over. It is the following:

Personality is applied to the bodies of those who were raised from the dead. Our Lord says, "Our friend Lazarus sleepeth: but I go that I may awake him out of sleep." And when He had prayed, "He cried with a loud voice, Lazarus, come forth and he that was dead, came forth." So also, at the time of the crucifixion, we read that "the graves were opened; and many bodies of the saints which slept arose, and went into the holy city, and appeared unto many.

In the light, therefore, of the above facts, namely, the distinction between that which is spiritual and that which is corporeal, the latter only being recognizable to the senses; the nature of man, as constituted of body and soul conjointly; the evidences of man's personal identity as such while living, and of the same in his resurrected state; and the proof of it furnished by what is recorded of some who were actually raised from the dead;—these facts, I submit, demonstrate the real, visible, corporeal, and therefore the literal resurrection of man.

Reverting once more to the great question before us— Will the second coming of Christ, when it does take place, be a purely spiritual, or a visible, corporeal, or personal coming? I remark that, in order to acquire an intelligent understanding of it, we must necessarily go back to the stones which compose the foundation on which we build.

One—and that the Lord Jesus Christ, "the chief corner-stone" thereof, has been already examined, as to what constitutes His complex Being, as "Emmanuel—God with us"—"God," as "manifest in the flesh." The result is, that He is presented to our view as possessed of the two component parts of proper humanity, namely, a material or corporeal body, and a reasonable soul.

A second stone in this foundation—of Christ's complex incarnate nature as our sin-atoning sacrifice, the "exceeding sorrow of His soul," and the crucifixion of His body on the cross, subjected him to an actual organic death, and He was buried in Joseph's tomb.

But, in this foundation is a third stone, to which I now for the first would call your special attention. It is this, that, whatever the Scriptures reveal, as to the mode or form of the second coming of Christ—whether it be spiritual or personal—the resurrection of Christ on the third day, according to His own word affords the only key to its solution. For it is clear that the resurrection of our Lord, if a purely spiritual one, could have had no connection whatever with that corporeal body in which He was born of the Virgin Mary, in which He labored, suffered, and died, and which, after His crucifixion, was laid in the sepulcher. On this hypothesis of the purely spiritual nature of Christ's resurrection, it may reasonably be demanded, what became of the entombed body of Christ after His resurrection? Was it cast aside as a thing of no account? Was it annihilated?

Suffice it to say, that it is but the fruit of that system of scriptural hermeneutics introduced into the Church in the early part of the third century by Origen, who, though a man of distinguished eminence in his day and generation, and of great apparent holiness and zeal, as he was also of profound scholarship; yet, having committed himself to the guidance of a fanciful imagination in his interpretations of Scripture, "was permitted of the Lord to be drawn away from the true sense of God's word, even while avowedly engaged in the study and exposition of it." The result to the Christian world for the most part from that day to the present has been, the substitution of the allegorical or spiritual, in the place of the literal, sense of Scripture, as the rule of interpretation. In its application to the subject in hand, it inevitably involves a denial of the resurrection of the material body of Christ, and hence affords a plausible pretext for the support of that theory which alleges that man, immediately after death, rises again in a purely spiritual state, in which he lives as a man, throughout eternity, either in heaven or hell.

The fallacy of this theory has been already exposed, in our definitions of the terms spiritual, corporeal, and personal, in proof of the complex nature of man, as constituted of a material body and a rational soul. And, having also demonstrated the scriptural doctrine of the perpetuity, intact, of man's personal identity after death, by and through the process of a literal resurrection of the body from the grave, and its reunion with the soul, I therefore argue that, if this is true of our personal identity of body and soul after death—on the principle that our blessed Lord and Savior Jesus Christ, though very God, was also truly and verily man; as He suffered death upon the cross, and was also buried, and rose again—so, His resurrection, in the mode or form of it, must also have been a real, visible, corporeal, and therefore a literal resurrection.

Let us, however, enter here a little into detail. As preliminary to what is to follow, I observe, that as "in all things it behooved Christ to be made like unto His brethren," during His life, ministry, sufferings, betrayal, trial, death, burial, and resurrection, as the Man Christ Jesus," He must have possessed their entire complex nature, corporeal and spiritual, in all its integrity, sin excepted; or, if "the soul" only "is the man"—if "the soul" only was raised from the dead, it follows that Christ is only half a Savior that while He atoned for the sin of man's soul, He left the body to be consigned to an eternal sleep that the inspired Paul committed an unpardonable blunder, and imposed upon the credulity of his Thessalonian brethren, when he prayed that their "whole body and soul and spirit might be preserved blameless unto the coming of our Lord Jesus Christ." But, as evidence of the fallacy of these hypotheses, in His proper personality, as constituted of body and soul (equally as when he conversed, and walked, and ate, and slept, and sorrowed, and rejoiced, and performed His many miraculous "deeds and wonders among men"), He predicted:

1. His own death by crucifixion. "And they shall scourge Him, and put Him to death." "And the Son of Man shall be betrayed unto the chief priests and unto the scribes...and to the Gentiles to mock, and to scourge, and to crucify Him." (Matthew 20:17ff).

2. That prediction was literally fulfilled. "The chief priests, and the rulers, and the people, cried out all at once, saying, away with this man...and they cried, saying, crucify Him, crucify Him!" "Then Pilate delivered Him to be crucified." "And they led Him away to crucify Him." And He (Jesus), bearing His cross, went forth into a place called the place of a skull...Golgotha, where they crucified him."

3. He was buried. "And after this, Joseph of

Arimathea (being a disciple of Jesus)...besought Pilate that he might take the body of Jesus: and Pilate gave him leave...Now, in the place where He was crucified, there was a garden: and in the garden a new sepulcher, wherein was never man yet laid. There laid they Jesus;" i.e., the corpse, or body, of Jesus. For we read that "Joseph took it down, and wrapped it in linen, and laid it in a sepulcher hewn in stone."

Now then, having proved that the personality of Christ, whom "it behooved to be made like unto His brethren," consisted of His endowment of a material body and a rational soul; and that His soul did not and could not either die or be raised; it follows that in order to preserve that personality in its integrity, the same body of Christ that was buried in the sepulcher must have risen, and must have been reunited to His soul.

4. That it was predicted of Christ, that it should so be. David, personifying Christ prophetically, says, "My flesh shall rest in hope. For thou wilt not leave my soul in hell" (i.e., the place of the departed), "neither wilt thou suffer thine Holy One to see corruption." Both Peter and Paul quote these words of David as prophetic of Christ's resurrection, declaring that "God raised Him up, having loosed the pains of death, because it was not possible that He should be holden of it." "David," says Paul, saw corruption: but He whom God raised up saw no corruption." And so also, Jesus Himself declared, "I have power to lay down my life, and I have power to take it again." And he predicted, "I will destroy this temple" (meaning His body), "and in three days I will raise it again." This, therefore, brings us to the direct . question.

5. Were these several predictions verified, by the actual resurrection of the same body of Christ from the dead, that was crucified on the cross? And if so, what evidence have we of it?

Now, we take the affirmative of this question, in the advocacy of the literal, in opposition to the so-called spiritual or metaphorical, resurrection of Christ. The evidence in support of such a claim, I admit, must be expressed, positive, leaving no room for further doubt, or it is of no value. In adducing this evidence, therefore, I refer you:

(1.) To the action taken by the enemies of Christ, regarding His dead body. Calling to mind the "deceiver's" predicted resurrection of Himself on "the third day;" and to protect the sepulcher against His thieving disciples; having obtained leave of Pilate, the scribes and pharisees "made sure the sepulcher, sealing a stone, and setting a watch." My purpose in referring to this fact is, simply to prove that the Jews understood a "resurrection from the dead" to mean a "resurrection of the body." The design of the above procedure, however, was to prove that Christ was an impostor. But, behold, at the end of the third day, an earthquake ministers to a celestial visitor from heaven, in rolling away the sealed stone from the mouth of the tomb, while the sentinels, overpowered with fear, become as dead men. Some of this same "watch," on their recovery, "went into the city, and showed unto the chief priests all the things that were done." And they not only believed that Christ had actually risen; but the bribery of the soldiers by the chief priests, to say that Christ's disciples came by night and stole Him away while they slept, is proof that they also believed it. For, if these soldiers were awake at the time of the alleged act, why did they thus suffer the corpse to be removed? And if they were asleep, how could they tell that it was stolen? Alas! Their "last error was worse than the first."

(2.) The next evidence of this fact is the testimony of some who had themselves been raised from the dead. "They came out of their graves after the resurrection, and went into the holy city, and appeared unto many."

(3.) But, I am now about to refer you to the most astounding moral phenomenon known in the history of man. I refer to the incredulity of Christ's own disciples, as to the fact of His actual, literal resurrection from the dead. Now, when we reflect that these men had been associated with Christ for more than three years; that they had listened to, and believed in, His doctrines; that they had witnessed his miracles (especially those connected with His raising several from the dead; e.g., the young maid of Cyrophenicia, and Lazarus who had lain in the grave four days); that they had heard Him predict His resurrection from the dead on the third day; and that they had all professed the most firm adhesion to Him and His cause in life and in death: I say, when we reflect on all this, how reasonable is it to infer that they would have awaited, in the exercise of a strong faith and unflinching hope, the approach of the resurrection morn, to hail with joy their risen Master!

But, so far from this, their conduct throughout evidenced an apparent determination, at all hazards, to prove that Christ was an impostor! But, under God, this very circumstance is made to furnish the only evidence demonstrative of the fact of Christ's literal resurrection. This will appear most conspicuous in every event which furnished them with the proof that "the Lord is risen indeed." The nature of the evidence demanded by them was of the highest order. In the case before us, that evidence may be gathered from the following facts, namely, first, the eleven disciples first doubted the credibility of those who reported that Christ was actually risen. Second, when they could no longer resist this evidence, they then doubted the reality of the appearance of Christ, which was declared to have been seen. And, to this, third, tangible evidence must be added, before all the eleven would admit the fact.

If therefore it can be shown, that all these species of evidence were afforded them in proof of Christ's literal resurrection from the dead, it will place that fact beyond the reach of further controversy. You will here again bear in mind, however, that in speaking of the resurrection of the same body of Christ from the grave that was crucified on the cross, I speak of that body as changed. In what that change consisted, must be a subject of after consideration. I now conduct you back to the sepulcher. It is at "the end of the Sabbath" (Jewish), as it merged into the opening dawn of "the first day of the week," the morning of the resurrection, and hence, the Christian Sabbath. At the mouth of the open sepulcher—for the great stone had been rolled away—stood a solitary female mourner. It was Mary Magdalene. She had come "while it was yet dark," seeking the body of Jesus.

But, behold, it was gone! And, still incredulous as to the fact of Christ's resurrection, even she, supposing the body to have been stolen, ran to bear the sad tidings to Peter and John, "They have taken away the Lord (meaning His body) out of the sepulcher, and we know not where they have laid Him." To satisfy themselves on this point, both these disciples ran to the sepulcher, and looking in, saw nothing but the shroud and napkin of the dead body. Peter, however, still remained incredulous. John only, believed that He was risen.

But, what, meanwhile, became of Mary Magdalene? Why, being now joined by "Joanna, and Mary the mother of James, and other women with them," she returned to the sepulcher to weep there. Yes, women were last at the cross, and first at the sepulcher. And now, added to the previous witnesses of Christ's resurrection, namely, His enemies the sepulchral sentinels, and the risen dead, we add:

(4.) The testimony of the angels, who to these weeping and "perplexed" female disciples of Christ, said, "Fear not ye: for I know that ye seek Jesus, who was crucified. He is not here: for He is risen, as He said. Come, see the place where the Lord (that is, the body) lay."

(5.) As last at the cross and the first at the tomb of Christ, these women are the first of His disciples to proclaim His resurrection to others.

Obedient to the angelic command, these women at once went their way quickly to His disciples as heralds of His resurrection. But, "their words seemed to them as idle tales, and they believed them not." No. With them the above evidence was not sufficient. Though they personally knew these witnesses, and had every reason to confide in their veracity, yet they doubted the credibility of these reports. They had been furnished with the first species of evidence in this matter. But it had proved entirely unsatisfactory.

They demanded, second, a visual demonstration of the fact. This, we must admit, was reasonable. For they well might, and indeed must have argued, "If risen, where is He? Has He, like Enoch or Elijah of old, been escorted to heaven, without having afforded His anxious, trembling, desponding disciples that evidence so essential to a proof of the fact, that of His having been seen?"

If so, this had been a direct violation of a promise made by Christ to them before His crucifixion. "After I am risen again, I will go before you into Galilee." But no. This could not be. And I now proceed to the evidence, that our blessed Lord, after His resurrection, appeared visibly, not only to one, but to many persons: not only in one, but in several places.

1. The first person by whom he was seen, was Mary Magdalene. As she stood weeping at the sepulcher, still in doubt as to His actually having risen, Jesus spoke to her. But she, supposing it was the gardener, said, "If ye have borne Him away, tell me where ye have laid Him, and I will take Him away. Jesus saith unto her, Mary!" It was enough. She exclaimed, "Rabboni."

2. After this, as Mary and the other women were on their way to Galilee to bear the joyful tidings to their brethren, "Jesus met them, saying, All hail! And they came and held Him by the feet, and worshiped Him. Then said Jesus unto them, Be not afraid: go tell my brethren that they go into Galilee, and there shall they see me." Accordingly, "Mary Magdalene cometh to tell the disciples that she had seen the Lord." Still, they were incredulous. "And they, when they heard that He was alive, and had been seen by her, believed not."

3. The risen Christ was next seen by the two disciples, who were on their way to Emmaus. To these,

though "their eyes" at first "were holden, that they should not know Him," that they might stand self-convicted of their "slowness of heart to believe all that the prophets had spoken" concerning Christ; yet "their eyes were" finally "opened, and they knew Him; and He vanished out of their sight."

Nor is the circumstance to be overlooked, that Christ made Himself known to these two disciples in the "breaking of bread," thereby showing, that though risen from the dead, He was still possessed of real corporeity. Yes, to a conviction of their judgment by reason, was added a conviction of their senses. They saw Christ eat before them. No doubt as to His literal resurrection found any further place in their minds. And hence, returning to Jerusalem, they at once made known these things to "the eleven disciples, and those that were with them, saying, The Lord is risen indeed."

4. "And, as they thus spake, Jesus stood in the midst of them" (i.e., the eleven), "and said unto them, Peace be unto you." The circumstances connected with this personal appearance of Christ to the eleven, introduces us to the third kind of evidence demanded by them, before they would believe.

When these disciples could no longer resist the credibility of the reports of Christ's resurrection by those who had seen Him, they then doubted the reality of the appearance of Christ to them. Hence, upon our Lord's presenting Himself in their midst, we read that "they were terrified and affrighted, and supposed that they had seen a spirit." This is a proof of their determination to reject all previous evidence, unless fortified by what was tangible.

Our Lord knew this. And therefore "He said unto them, Why are ye troubled? And why do thoughts arise in your hearts? Behold my hands and my feet: it is I myself. Handle me, and see: for a spirit hath not flesh and bones, as ye see me have."...Besides, He "partook of their broiled fish, and did eat before them."

5. But, on this occasion, "Thomas, one of the twelve, was not with them, when Jesus came." Eight days after, however, Thomas being present, "came Jesus, the doors being shut, and stood in the midst of them, and said, Peace be unto you." This occasion of Christ's appearance furnished the opportunity for the dissipation of the last lingering doubt, as to the reality of His resurrection. "The other disciples had said to Thomas, We have seen the Lord." Now, mark. They did not declare to him whether or not they had handled the body of Christ. My own impression is, that they had not. This I think is borne out by the recorded effect of Christ's challenge to them, "Handle me," which is, that "they believed not for joy, and wondered." Surely, the above demonstrations of the fact were sufficient to produce convictions in their minds without it. But, if their declaration as above to Thomas, "We have seen the Lord," was still accompanied with a lingering doubt in any of their minds, the result of the declared incredulity of that disciple set it at rest forever. He said, "Except I shall see in His hands the prints of the nails, and put my finger into the print of the nails, and thrust my hand into His side, I will not believe." Yes, the evidence of the sense of touch, with him, must be added to that of sight, before he will be convinced. The condescending Savior therefore says to him, "Thomas, reach hither thy finger, and behold my

hands: and reach hither thy hand, and thrust it into my side: and be not faithless, but believing!"

And now, what could the doubting Thomas do, but yield and he did yield. In holy faith and worshipful adoration he exclaimed, "My Lord, and my God!"

I only add to the above that, as we have no account that any one of the disciples informed Jesus of the declaration made by the unbelieving Thomas, either before or after He entered the chamber where they were assembled; and as He entered that chamber while the doors were closed, without divesting Himself of that glorified body which had been recently raised from the tomb; taken in connection with the above evidence of His actual literal resurrection; we are furnished with a demonstration beyond which nothing can be demanded or given, of the personal identity, divine and human, of our blessed Savior Jesus Christ, by a reunion of his body and soul, in his resurrected estate.

And now, in conclusion, the risen Christ, having subsequently appeared to the eleven disciples while engaged in fishing on the sea of Tiberias; then to the five hundred brethren on a mountain in Galilee; and once more to the eleven, when He gave them their commission and sent them forth to preach the Gospel; and having "been seen of them forty days, and speaking to them of the things pertaining to the kingdom of God;" in that same body in which He was born of the Virgin Mary, and which was crucified, and was buried, and was raised again on the third day:—in that same body, but changed, "while the disciples beheld, He was taken up" into heaven, "and a cloud received Him out of their sight."

This then, that is, the corporeal, visible, personal, but

changed and glorified mode or form in which Christ was raised from the dead, and in which he ascended to Heaven, will be the mode or form in which he will return.

CHAPTER 5

Evidence of Christ's Glorified Humanity

W e shall select, as the basis of an illustration of this subject, the following passage, 2 Peter 1:16, 17. "For we have not followed cunningly devised fables, when we made known unto you the power and coming of our Lord and Savior Jesus Christ, but were eye-witnesses of His Majesty. For He received of God the Father honor and glory, when there came to Him such a voice from the excellent glory, "This is my beloved Son, in whom I am well pleased."

This is a subject that may well be placed in the category of "the deep things" of God's revealed mysteries—the "some things hard to be understood" of Paul, and which, as we have seen, on the principle of the allegorizing or spiritualizing theory of interpretation, "they that are unlearned and unstable wrest, as they do also the other scriptures." Our prayer is, that it may not be "to their own destruction; the eyes of their understanding being enlightened, they may know what is the hope of their calling, and what the riches of the glory of their inheritance in the saints."

Nor is the subject of our present inquiry to be classed with those "foolish and unlearned questions" which, "engendering strifes," we are called upon to "avoid." Still, while meditating on what "the wisdom of God" has been graciously pleased to reveal to us in these premises, we would not forget that it is "a mystery," which, like the river disclosed to Ezekiel in prophetic vision, issuing from under the threshold of the temple, gradually expands into a width that "cannot be passed over." While, however, we are not presumptuously to intrude into those "secret things which belong alone to the Lord our God," we are not to be deterred from a diligent and prayerful investigation of "the things that are revealed to us and our children"—"the things which the angels desire to look into."

The subject then in hand, relates to the nature of the resurrected humanity of Christ. In reference to it, I remark,

1. Negatively, that it was not a spiritual resurrection. This could not be. The body of our Lord that was interred in the sepulcher, was material. And matter even when attenuated to its utmost capacity, cannot be transformed into that which is purely spiritual, or incorporeal. And, could it have been so transformed, as Christ was also possessed of a reasonable or spiritual soul, this spiritual resurrected body would have become so absorbed into, and so identified with, his material body, as to have destroyed all personality. Besides, it would involve the dilemma, that Christ had two spiritual human natures which is an absurdity. But, take a view of the subject.

2. Positively. And here I must premise, as necessary to an intelligent view of the matter, that we must distinguish between a purely spiritual body, and a body spiritualized.

The former consists of a being immaterial, incorporeal, and hence, not tangible to the senses. That is, it can be neither seen nor handled. On the other hand, a body spiritualized, is a material substance changed, or transformed from a lower to a higher state, thereby adapting it to a new, and a more exalted and glorious sphere of action. And if this be so, a body may be spiritualized or changed, without ceasing to be material. Such a body, however refined or transparent it may become, does not necessarily lose its inherent elements of corporeity. On any other hypothesis, personal identity, so essential to the whole man, as I have just said, would be destroyed.

Now, apply this principle to our blessed Lord and Savior Jesus Christ, and I argue that, as neither His body alone, nor His soul alone, but both conjointly, made up His whole manhood, unless the same material body that was crucified and buried was also raised, and reunited to His soul, His manhood or personal identity was not sustained in its integrity. But, as has been already abundantly demonstrated, that same body of Christ that was crucified and buried in, also emerged from, the tomb, on the third day. Yes, and by the act of the resurrection power of God, it was also changed. Christ's mortal body, as "the first-fruits of them that slept," at that instant "put on immortality." And, as I shall now proceed to prove, when Christ's body was raised from the dead, it consisted, not in being a purely spiritual, but, in being:

3. A spiritualized body. That is, it was changed. In treating of this deep mystery of God, however, let me not awaken expectations beyond what was designed. I do not mean to venture into this shoreless and fathomless ocean

beyond my depth. I would also scrupulously avoid all metaphysical subtleties and amusing speculations regarding it. I say, then: of the mode of the hidden process by which the dead body of Christ was both raised and changed; in other words, how the material was spiritualized, we know nothing. And, of the actual nature and qualities of that spiritualized body, we know but "in part." A thick film spreads over the "glass" through which we are now compelled to look at it. And hence, under the most favorable circumstances, it is a much easier task to tell in what it does not, than in what it does, consist. To this method, then (at least in part), I shall resort, in my endeavors to illustrate this subject.

That Christ's body, when raised, and changed, did not become angelic. "He took not on him the nature of angels"—and, unless He lost His entire personal identity in passing through the grave to His resurrected state—which we have proved an impossibility—He must have retained, after His resurrection, that same nature, in which He died and was buried. Now if, before His resurrection, His nature was not angelic, how, I ask, could it become so after that event?

The advocates of the theory of Christ's spiritual resurrection, have labored to support it on the ground of an alleged exact correspondence between the nature of Christ's raised body, and that of the angels. But this theory, while it is in direct contradiction to the inspired Pauline statement as above, that Christ "took not on Him the nature of angels," rests on the assumption that "angels," in their nature, are incorporeal or purely spiritual beings. This, however, is contrary to fact. This can only be said to be true of the two Persons in the infinite and eternal Godhead—

the Father and the Holy Ghost. We are to bear in mind, that "angels," whatever be their nature, are created beings. And creation is the great boundary-line which separates between that which is purely spiritual, as the Invisible Godhead, and that which is corporeal, as angels and men. If it be urged, but angels are called "spirits,"—"who maketh his angels spirits;" I reply, in the same passage we read, "and his ministers a flame of fire." Here, the terms "angels" and "ministers" denote the same thing. While, therefore, the term "spirits" may be understood to refer to the rational, the term, "a flaming fire," which we know to be a material element, is used to signify the corporeal vehicle, through which to manifest themselves. That their corporeity differs from the human, is admitted. It is of a vastly higher, more refined, and ethereal nature. But, it were as consistent to deny the materiality of the air we breathe, as, on this account, to deny angelic corporeity. Besides, the Scriptures abound with instances of visible and corporeal angelic visitations to men on earth, thereby illustrating the adaptedness of their compound nature, rational and corporeal, to answer the heaven-devised purposes of "ministering angels, sent forth to minister to them who shall be heirs of salvation."

Still, the nature of angels as thus defined, though corporeal, and that of the resurrected body of Christ, are not identical. The difference is this: their nature, as they are not subject to death, is not susceptible of any change. This is true, not only of "the elect," but of the "fallen angels." True, by their sin, they lost the holiness of their character. But we nowhere read of their dying. In the same nature in which they rebelled, "are they reserved in chains under darkness, against the day of judgment." It is this circumstance which renders their salvation an impossibility. Christ did not assume their nature. "But he took upon Him the seed of Abraham." That is, He assumed the grosser corporeity of human nature, which, having sinned, became subject also to death. But, in order to accomplish the great object of His mission into our world as "God manifest in the flesh" (which was, "to destroy him that had the power of death, that is, the Devil, and deliver them who through fear of death were all their lifetime subject to bondage"), "the Son of God" must die, not only, but rise again.

Now, as "an angel cannot be actually transformed into a human being without ceasing to be an angel;" so, by parity of reason, a material body cannot be actually transformed into the angelic, without ceasing to be human. It follows, that as our Divine Redeemer ("who in all things, sin excepted, it behooved to be made like unto us") suffered, died, and was buried in His proper human nature; so, when He rose from the dead, He must have risen in the same proper human nature. That He did so arise, is evident from the angel's declaration to the weeping Mary, at the sepulcher. "He (Christ) is not here. He is risen." "Behold the place where the Lord (i.e., the corpse) lay."

Nor, again, did the difference in the condition, between the body of Christ as crucified and buried, and of the same body as raised and changed, destroy His real corporeity. The question before us now, "as to the link that united God and man in one person, namely, Christ;" but it is as to the spiritualized nature of His risen body. And, however we may reason analogically from our resurrection, as illustrated by the dead seed sown and brought to life, in proof of the fact of the resurrection of Christ, at this point all coincidence between us and His ceases. In all things, He must have the preeminence. As, even in His death, "He saw no corruption," and which differs from that of the saints, who do see corruption; so, as "the first-fruits of them that sleep in Christ," our resurrection state is to be inferred from His, not His from ours. "Who shall change our vile body, and fashion it like unto His own glorious body."

But, notwithstanding the proofs of the actual corporeity of the raised and spiritualized body of our blessed Lord on the third day, the spiritualists would have us to believe that all these instances were mere visible illusions. We are told, that "an appearance generally denotes the opposite of reality." And so, when we read that "Christ appeared, to put away sin by the sacrifice of Himself;" it was a mere phantom! That when He said to Mary, "Touch me not," there was nothing to touch! And, that, when the women "worshiped" the risen Savior, "holding Him by the feet," they were actually clasping less than a shadow! Are you prepared to receive such teaching as this?

But, finally, on this topic of the spiritualized body of the risen Christ, with a view to obviate an alleged difficulty arising from our exposition, namely, that the same body of Christ that was raised from the dead ascended to heaven; it is contended by some, that while they admit a literal resurrection to have taken place on the third day, yet that our blessed Lord, when He left his disciples and ascended to heaven, laid aside that raised body, or in some way changed it into a purely spiritual body, totally distinct from that seen by His disciples after his resurrection.

This is argued from these facts. That there are a number of extraordinary circumstances and actions, connected with these visible manifestations of Christ, in His resurrected spiritualized body. For example: His appearing to Mary under the aspect of a gardener. His talking and eating, with His disciples, without being recognized in His true character. And His entering the room where the eleven were assembled, while the doors were closed. The question therefore is, how are these extraordinary circumstances and actions to be explained? Not, I submit, (as some allege) by his resurrected body undergoing a change; or by His assumption, alternately, of a material and ethereal form at will; or by a transformation of His risen spiritualized corporeity into different shapes to suit the occasion, from that with which He left the sepulcher. Doubtless, during the interval of the forty days that elapsed between the resurrection and the ascension, while the Savior was employed "in speaking" among His disciples "of the things pertaining to the kingdom of God," there was to them an eclipsing of the full glory of His beatified risen body, which, however, no more argued any change in the glorified body itself, than an eclipse of the natural sun in the heavens argues a change in its physical organism as the bright ruler of the day. The ostensible reason of this, on the part of the risen Savior was, that the time had not yet come for the full "restoration of the kingdom to Israel." A subordinate reason was, to produce in their minds a conviction of the reality of His resurrection, by appeals to their understanding, rather than by a brilliant display of His full glory to their senses. They had criminally forgotten "all that the prophets had spoken concerning Christ, how He should suffer, and die, and rise again on the third day." And, as we have seen, such was their "slowness of heart to believe" that He was actually risen, that they persistently refused to admit it, except on the highest evidence that could be given—that of tangible demonstration. It may well be doubted, therefore, whether the brightest instantaneous exhibit by Christ to them of His risen glorified humanity, would have led them to believe in and receive Him as such. Hence, while "He showed himself alive" to them "after His passion" as above recited, it was "by many infallible proofs," i.e., miracles, brought about, not on Himself, but on them. Take a single example in illustration. As our Lord was walking with the two disciples on their way to Emmaus, it is recorded of them, that " their eyes were holden, that they should not know Him." And so, He whose look was sufficient to remove the bolts and bars of closed doors, could also lock up the senses of the eleven against a perception of His presence, till He was seen standing in their midst. And, finally, if the Savior, before His crucifixion, to escape the stoning of the Jews, could "hide Himself," and yet pass by "through the midst of them out of the Temple;" surely we can have no difficulty as to His "vanishing" out of the sight of the two disciples, after that event.

Regarding the changed or spiritualized body of our risen Redeemer by the power of God, (limited as is our knowledge of its nature), yet enough is revealed to us of its peculiar properties or qualities, to enable us to adopt the language of our text, and say, we have not followed cunningly devised fables in our endeavors to analyze it. Nor is the same veil that eclipsed its brightness during the brief sojourn of the risen Christ with the early Church, drawn over the present eye of faith.

An exemplification of this "glory" was made on the

mount of transfiguration. The humiliation of Christ was His transfiguration as "the word made flesh," with its accompaniments of poverty, obscurity, and suffering. On the other hand, the transfiguration on the mount, was an exhibit and earnest of His glorified risen humanity, and the power and splendor of His future reign. The design of it was, to furnish to the three disciples who witnessed it, a proof of His messiahship, and to fortify their minds against the influence of the shame of His life and death. But, how soon was this resplendent display of the glory of Christ obliterated from their minds! Their conduct, subsequently to the trial, crucifixion, and resurrection of their Divine Master, was evidence of this. And, as has been shown, even amid the "many infallible signs" afforded them of His resurrection glory, their perceptions of it were greatly obscured. Nor was this obscurity removed, till the descent of the Holy Spirit upon them on the day of Pentecost. Then, "all things," which Christ either did or said respecting Himself, or which had been said of Him by the prophets, "were brought to their remembrance." Hence, thirty-five years after the transfiguration on the mount, the apostle Peter writes, "We have not followed cunningly devised fables, when we made known unto you the power and coming of Jesus Christ, but were eye-witnesses of His majesty. For He received from God the Father, honor and glory, when there came to Him such a voice from the excellent glory, this is my beloved Son, in whom I am well pleased."

Now, observe, that the apostle, in speaking of the incarnate Christ before His passion, declares that He "received of God the Father honor and glory," and immediately connects it with His transfiguration. The question then is, what was transfigured? And the answer is, the incarnate body of Christ. Otherwise, what meanwhile became of the material body of Christ? And, this transfiguration the apostle calls "the power and coming of our Lord and Savior Jesus Christ." Matthew, Mark, and Luke, in describing His appearance, tell us that "His countenance was altered;" that "His face did shine as the sun;" and that "His raiment was white as the light," "shining," "glistening," "exceeding white as the snow." Daniel, to whom He was revealed in prophetic vision in His resurrected "glory" as the Christ of God, says: "I beheld, till the Ancient of Days did sit, whose garment was white as snow, and the hair of His head like the pure wool." And so also the prophet Ezekiel, speaking of the Lord (Jehovah) in human form, says that, "upon the likeness of the throne was the likeness as the appearance of a man above upon it,"..."from the appearance of His loins even downward, fire: and from His loins even upward, as the appearance of brightness, as the color of amber." And, speaking of His voice, the same prophet says, that it was "like the noise of great waters, as the voice of the Almighty, the voice of speech, as the noise of an host." And "this," he adds, "was the appearance of the likeness of the glory of the Lord." Again we turn to the prophet Daniel, who says of Him, "Then I lifted up mine eyes and looked, and behold, a certain man"—referring to Christ's resurrected glorified humanity—"a certain man clothed in linen, whose loins were girded with fine gold of Uphaz; His body also was like the beryl, and His face as the appearance of lightning, and His eyes as lamps of fire, and His arms and His feet like in color to polished brass, and the voice of His words like the voice of a multitude." Finally, we turn to the Revelator John, who says of Him, "And I turned to see the voice that spake with me. And being turned, I saw seven golden candlesticks: and in the midst of the seven candlesticks one like unto the Son of Man, clothed with a garment down to the foot, and girt to the breasts with a golden girdle. His head and hairs white like wool, white as snow; and His eyes as a flame of fire; and His feet like unto fine brass, as if they had been burned in a furnace; and His voice as the sound of many waters: and holding in His right hand seven stars: and out of His mouth a sharp two-edged sword proceeding: and His countenance as the sun shineth in his strength."

But, from this brief exhibit of the glory of the resurrected humanity of Christ, let us pass to a view of that same glory, as connected with, Divine Attributes. The effect of the above vision of Christ to John in His resurrected "glory" was, that he "fell at His feet as dead." It is not our purpose to enter here into a proof and defense of the proper Deity of Christ in detail. That necessity is avoided by the very attributes claimed by our Lord, in His address to His servant John on the above occasion. He laid His right hand upon him and said, "Fear not, I am the first, and the last: I am He that liveth, and was dead; and, behold, I am alive forevermore, Amen: and have the keys of hell and of death."

Of the identity of Christ as above, with "the Son of Man" who was revealed in the visions of Daniel and Ezekiel, there can be no doubt. The 8th verse of this chapter may be taken as expository of the attributes claimed by Christ in the passage just quoted. Said He, "I am Alpha and Omega, the beginning and the ending, saith the Lord, which is, and which was, and which is to come, the Almighty." These titles, therefore, namely, "the first and the last," or their equivalent, "the Alpha and Omega," being the first and last letters of the Greek alphabet (and which are also used as numerals), are designed to signify the eternity of the Being who claims them.

Now, of "the Almighty God," said Isaiah, "Who hath wrought and done it, calling the generations from the beginning? I, Jehovah, the first, and with the last, I am He."

But Paul declares concerning Christ, that "He is before all things," and that "by Him all things consist." That is, that Jesus Christ, as the Son of God, is "the Being through whom creation received its origin, and who conducts it through the ages of ages to its final destination."

Therefore, in this book (chapter 4:8), John applies the unutterable name of Jehovah to Christ, and which, in that passage, is a paraphrase of that name as used in the corresponding song of the Seraphim in the sixth chapter of Isaiah. We will compare John with Isaiah:

John says, "And the four living creatures rest not day and night, saying, Holy, Holy, Holy, Lord God Almighty, who is, and who was, and who is to come:" or who is the Coming One.

Isaiah says, The six-winged Seraphim cried one unto another, saying, Holy, Holy, Holy, is the Jehovah of hosts; the whole earth is full of His glory."

What a Name! It is expressive of the summing up of all existence, in all time and mood, in His own infinite Being, which is of all existence the source and center, and of life, past, present, and to come, the all-comprehensive, all-sustaining ocean!

Such, then, are the attributes of the resurrected and ascended Personal Christ. It only remains that we notice, His resurrected official dignity. This is threefold. It relates:

1. To Christ's intercession in our behalf at the right hand of God. In His humiliation Christ appeared as a Prophet. Now that He is risen and glorified, He appears in heaven as a Priest, to intercede for us. "But this man, after He had offered one sacrifice for sins, forever sat down on the right hand of God." "Wherefore He is able also to save them to the uttermost that come unto God by Him, seeing He ever liveth to make intercession for them. For, such an High Priest became us, who is holy, harmless, undefiled, separate from sinners, and made higher than the heavens." This intercession of Christ on our behalf extends from the time of the ascension to the period when He shall descend from heaven.

2. As our Judge. This is the second official work of the risen Christ in his resurrected human nature. Thus, the apostle says, "and He commanded us to preach unto the people, and to testify, that it is He which was ordained of God to be the judge of quick and dead;" "because He hath appointed a day, in which He will judge the world in righteousness, by that man whom He hath ordained." And, as such, He will judge the fallen angels, who are "reserved in chains, under darkness, against the day of judgment." Also Antichrist, "the man of sin" and "son of perdition," whom He will "consume with the spirit of his mouth, and destroy with the brightness of His coming." And He will also judge the poor, and all their wicked oppressors. "He will judge the poor of the people, He will save the children of the needy,

and He will break in pieces the oppressor." "He will not judge after the sight of His eyes, neither reprove after the hearing of His ears; but with righteousness shall He judge the poor, and reprove with equity for the meek of the earth; and He will smite the earth with the rod of His mouth, and with the breath of His lips shall He slay the wicked." And, finally, connected with Christ's dignity as risen, is:

3. His office as King. Isaiah, in predicting of Him, says, "He shall be called,...the Prince of Peace." He is elsewhere styled "the Prince of the kings of the earth." Hence, as David's son, who is to sit upon His throne, He was born a king," "The king of the Jews." And, at His first coming, had they received Him as such, He had then established Himself on David's throne. But, "by the determinate counsel and foreknowledge of God, they, with wicked hands, crucified and slew Him." And now, see the wisdom of God in all this. Christ's rejection by the Jews, opens the door for His expiating human guilt by the sacrifice of Himself on the cross; and for His burial, resurrection, and ascension to heaven, whither He has gone to receive a kingdom, and to return."

The Revelator John says, "And I saw heaven opened, and behold, a white horse; and He that sat upon him was called faithful and true, and in righteousness He doth judge and make war. His eyes were as a flame of fire, and on His head were many crowns. And He had a name written, that no man knew but Himself...And out of His mouth goeth a sharp sword, that with it He should smite the nations: and He shall rule them with a rod of iron: and He treadeth the wine-press of the fierceness of the wrath of God. And, He hath on His vesture, and on His thigh, a name written—

King of Kings, and Lord of Lords."

Blessed be God! "Behold, a King"—Jesus, in His risen and glorified humanity—"shall reign and prosper, and shall execute judgment and justice in the earth."

To relieve this important doctrine of Christ's second coming of all misapprehension, I propose to present it in the following syllogistic aspects, namely: That can only be restored to the Church, which has been withdrawn from the Church. But the spiritual presence of Christ never has been withdrawn from the Church.

Therefore, the spiritual presence of Christ is not the thing to be restored to the Church at the second advent. But the personal presence of Christ, at His ascension, was withdrawn from the Church. Therefore, the personal presence of Christ is the thing to be restored to the church at the second advent.

I have, on a previous occasion, considered those passages which distinguish between the immaterial or spiritual, and hence invisible essence of the first and third persons of the Infinite God head—the Father and the Holy Spirit—"whom no man hath seen nor can see;" and the visible manifestations of the same eternal Godhead to man, in the person of the Immaculate Jesus, "the Word made flesh," "Emmanuel, God with us," and of whom John, who saw Him, bare witness, "This is the true God, and eternal life."

I have also explained the sense in which the Scriptures represent Christ's spiritual coming to His people. I now refer you to several passages which distinguish between the fellowship which His people hold with Christ in virtue of this spiritual presence, during His intercession on their behalf "at the right hand of the majesty in the heavens;"

and His visible appearing "the second time, without sin, unto salvation." Thus, the apostle exhorts the Corinthians to see that they come behind in no gift;" for, inasmuch as "God is faithful, by whom they were called" (i.e., by the Spirit) "unto the fellowship of His Son Jesus Christ our Lord, He would also confirm them unto the end, that they might be blameless in the Day of our Lord Jesus Christ; and this he urges as a motive for their constant waiting for the coming of our Lord Jesus Christ." Here, clearly, while the "coming" spoken of was to them, future; the spiritual "fellowship" was to them, present.

This brings us to another stand-point, absolutely indispensable to a proper understanding of the subject in hand. It is this: That all the prophecies of Scripture which speak of Christ, relate exclusively to His humanity, either in His suffering, or His glorified estate. They point us to His suffering estate. And here we are directed, 1. To His parentage. As the "seed" of the woman, He was to be "born of a virgin," "of the house and lineage of David." 2. To His birthplace—Bethlehem. 3. To the scene of His personal ministry—"The land of Zebulun, and the land of Nephthalim." 4. To His prophetic and priestly functions. The first, as the great "Teacher sent from God:" and the second, as a sin-atoning sacrifice; and hence, they point us also: 5. To His death. To this end, "a body was prepared Him," in which He "bare our sins on a tree," thereby procuring for us "peace," "reconciliation," "sanctification," and free access into the holiest of all, "in the body of His flesh through death."

But, in connection with the prophetic and priestly offices of Christ, the Scriptures also speak of His kingly or regal prerogatives, all of which relate to His glorified humanity. And here, permit me again to remark, that the Deity, abstractedly considered—the Deity, considered in reference to His ineffable, spiritual essence, cannot be the subject of prophecy. He is only such as "Deity manifest in the flesh." And the class of prophecies now under consideration—those relating to Christ's kingly or regal prerogatives—all stand directly connected with His second coming, in His estate of glorified humanity.

Accordingly, it will be found that the prophetic Scriptures specify with the greatest minuteness the details of that event. They point out the place of His descent; the seat of His Government; the extent of His Dominion; the happiness of His subjects; the duration of His reign; and the time, both when He will commence His millennial reign, and when it will terminate, by the delivering up of that kingdom to the Father.

The only point which at present concerns us, however, is the office of Christ as King. In this capacity it was predicted of Him, that "He shall be great, and shall be called the Son of the Highest, and that the Lord God shall give unto Him the throne of His father David." For, "God had sworn by an oath unto David, that, of the fruit of his loins according to the flesh" (not according to the spirit), "He would raise up Christ to sit on his throne." It is however urged by many, that as the sitting of Christ on David's throne was to follow His resurrection, He commenced His kingly reign as David's son immediately on His ascension to heaven. Hence the foundation of the popular idea, that Christ now reigns as King over His saints; in support of which, the two following passages are quoted: "Sit Thou on my right hand, until I make thy foes thy footstool." And, "He must reign, till He hath put all enemies under His feet." But, I submit, as the first passage has reference to the exercise of Christ's office in heaven as the intercessor of His people "till" His and their enemies are subdued unto Him; so the last regards His providential government over the kings and nations of the earth, till "the kingdoms of this world are become the kingdom of our Lord and of His Christ."

To the above I add that, if Christ, at the time of His ascension, sat on David's throne, it follows, that there are two thrones in heaven. For Paul tells us that our Lord, upon His return to heaven, "sat down on the right hand of the throne of God." At least, this result follows, unless it can be shown that the phrases, "throne of David" and "throne of God" are convertible terms. But, that they are not, and that our blessed Lord has not yet taken possession of "the throne of His father David," the apostle Peter most explicitly declares respecting "the patriarch David, that he is both dead and buried, and that his sepulcher (not his throne) is with us unto this day." And, as though this were not sufficient, the same apostle adds, that "David is not ascended into the heavens." How, then, I ask, can his throne be there?

In conclusion, therefore, on this subject, I remark, that when Christ ascended to heaven, and sat down on the throne of God, it was not to commence His reign as king, but to exercise His office as our intercessor. Hence says Paul, "Now, of the things which we have spoken, this is the sum: We have such an High Priest, who is set on the right hand of the throne of the majesty in the heavens, whose office-work now is, not to reign over His people as King, for He has not yet "received his kingdom;" but, to make perpetual intercession for us.

The sum of the whole matter, then, is simply this: David has no throne in heaven. And Christ, though born a king, and crucified as a king—"the King of the Jews"—yet, "the kingdom, and dominion, and greatness of the kingdom under the whole heaven, has never yet been given to Him or to His saints. But, there stands the immutable oath of God to David, that Christ, as his Son "according to the flesh"—mark, not according to the spirit—"shall sit on His throne."

It follows inevitably, that when this oath is verified to David, it must be by Christ's sitting on David's throne at the commencement of the millennium.

I now observe, that the New Testament scriptures harmonize with the old, on the subject of Christ's second coming being personal. Seeing that it is only in His human nature, that the Savior can be said to "come," to "appear," to be "sent;" the phrase, the "coming of the Son of Man," inasmuch as He is always spiritually present with His people, must involve a visible, personal coming. For example: That the following and similar passages—"Waiting for the coming of the Lord Jesus Christ,"—"and to wait for His Son from heaven,"—"Blessed is that servant whom His Lord, when He cometh, shall find watching," all denote a visible and personal coming, is evident from the following:

In the New Testament there are three nouns substantively used to signify that event, the first of which is *revelation*; the second, *appearance*; and the third, *coming*, or *presence*.

Now, though the word *revelation* may be employed to signify the discovery of spiritual truth to the mind, yet it is never so applied in reference either to the first or second coming of Christ. As it regards the last-named event, in the sense of uncovering, revelation, disclosure, display, it occurs in the following passages: "Waiting for the revelation of Jesus Christ." "At the revelation of Jesus Christ, with His mighty angels." "Might be found unto praise, and honor, and glory, at the revelation of Jesus Christ." "Hope for the grace that is brought unto you, at the revelation of Jesus Christ."

The second term signifying *appearance, display, splendor*, i.e., "the appearance of a thing corporeal and resplendent,"— occurs in relation to Christ's second coming, in the following passages: "Until the appearing of our Lord Jesus Christ." "Who shall judge the quick and the dead, at His appearing and kingdom." "Unto them that love His appearing." "Looking for that blessed hope, the glorious appearing of the great God, even our Savior, Jesus Christ."

The third term which signifies *presence, coming*, occurs, in all, twenty-five times. Now if, when this word is applied to others than the Savior, it can mean, and is admitted to mean nothing short of a personal coming, with what consistency, I ask, can it be interpreted to mean quite a different thing when applied to Him?

In the following passages, it is applied to different individuals: "I am glad of the coming of Stephanus." "God...who comforted me by the coming of Titus." "And not by his coming only." "But his—i.e., Paul's—bodily presence is weak." "That your rejoicing may be more abundant in Christ Jesus for me, by my coming to you." "Wherefore, my beloved, as ye have always obeyed, not as in my presence only, but now much more in my absence." And, in the following passage, the same word is applied to the last antichrist, who, both before and since the time of the Reformation, has been regarded as the *Papistico-Infidel Leader* of iniquity, who was to appear in the last "perilous times" to come. "And that man of sin be revealed, whose coming is after the manner of Satan." Yes. As Jesus Christ, as "God manifest in the flesh," was the embodied visible personification of all good; so Satan, through this incarnate "son of perdition," at the close of "the times of the Gentiles," will be the embodied visible personification of all evil.

I pass now to those passages—in all, seventeen, where the word for coming is applied to the second coming of Christ. "What is the sign of thy coming." "As the lightning... so shall the coming of the Son of Man be." "As the days of Noah, so shall also the coming of the son of man be." "Till the flood came so shall the coming of the son of man be." "They that are Christ's at His coming." "What is our hope... are not even ye, in the presence of our Lord Jesus Christ at His coming?" "To the end that He may establish your hearts unblamable...at the coming of our Lord." "We which remain unto the coming of our Lord." "And I pray God your whole body and soul be preserved blameless unto the coming of our Lord Jesus Christ." "Now we beseech you, brethren, by the coming of our Lord." "That wicked"— the last personal Antichrist—"whom the Lord shall destroy with the brightness of His coming." "Be patient, therefore, brethren, unto the coming of the Lord." "For the coming of the Lord draweth nigh." "We made known unto you the power and coming, of our Lord Jesus Christ." Peter here alludes to the transfiguration on the mount, which was personal and visible. "Where is the promise of His coming?" "Looking for, and hasting unto the coming of the day of God." "And now, little children, abide in Him... and not be ashamed before Him at His coming."

In the view, therefore, of all that has been offered on the subject of the mode or form in which the second coming of Christ will transpire, I think we may affirm, without either breach of modesty or fear of refutation, that, when that long-predicted event does take place—a prediction reaching back to the time of "Enoch, the seventh generation from Adam,"—it can be understood of none other than a real, visible, personal coming. That "same Jesus," which was "taken up" from earth to heaven forty days after His resurrection, in His glorified human body, "shall," with the same body, "so come again in like manner."

"Spirit of Grace" through Thine enlightening, regenerating, and sanctifying power, may we all "love His appearing," and "be accounted worthy to stand before the Son of Man."

CHAPTER 6

Summary of Millenarianism

The contents of this chapter embraces also such parts of the subject matter in the "reply" which follows, as was deemed necessary to complete the synopsis. The various theories of anti- and post-millenarians on the subject of the second personal coming of Christ and the millennium, as the discussions in this treatise show, are based upon a series of negatives. We claim to have historically demonstrated upon the authority of "Holy Scripture and ancient authors," that the millenarian scheme is founded upon and derived from the prophetic announcements of the Old Testament prophets, and of Christ and His apostles, and that it was believed in and became universally prevalent among the orthodox as the Catholic faith of the Church during the early post-apostolic age. Also, that it met with no opposition, until the substitution of the allegorical in the place of the literal interpretations of "the teachings of Isaiah and John concerning the second coming of Christ," as introduced into the Church by Origen in the early part of the third century.

Now, it was this unauthorized change in the original law prescribed for the interpretation of "the Messianic prophecies," which necessitated those who adopted it to frame their respective exegesis in such wise as to stand out in antagonism to the literal interpretation of the prophecies regarding the coming and kingdom of Christ, as taught by the primitive chiliasts [a thousand years]. In analogy to the future assault upon the pre-existing "camp of the saints and the beloved city" by the post-millennial "Gog and Magog" hosts, the citadel of the pre-Christian Jewish, apostolic, and early primitive millenarians, has been the object of attack, on widely different grounds, by its anti and post-millenarian opponents. Hence, in accordance with the rule of Tertullian—"that which is first is true, that which is later is adulterate"—the advocates of millenarianism have occupied the position of the defensive against the objections of its assailants of every name. Again: Whatever may be said of the variations that have obtained among literalists, in their interpretations of "the teachings of Isaiah and John concerning the second coming of Christ," yet, compared with the numerous contradictory theories of the allegorists, we submit, we are furnished with a strong presumptive argument in behalf of the former. For, differ as they may in some of the minor details of the millenarian scheme, literalists, ancient, medieval, and modern, have always substantially maintained the same great fundamental tenets required by the law of their adoption. On the other hand, the allegorists, surrendering themselves to the caprice of fancy, have originated theories between no two of which can be traced the remotest resemblance.

Take, for example, the ancient theories of Origen,

Eusebius, and Augustine. Or take the more modern theories of Grotius, Prideaux, Vint, and Bush, and of the Millerites, together with that based upon the popular interpretations of Matthew 24:27–30, and of the Whitbyan "New Hypothesis" as founded upon Revelation 20:1–6: and who, we deferentially ask, will venture to affirm that a law of interpretation of "the Messianic prophecies" such as that adopted by the allegorists, could by a possibility have been given by inspiration from God? This would be to argue that The Law of sacred hermeneutics given by the Holy Spirit, instead of "guiding us into all truth," was designed to allure us into a wilderness of uncertainty and conjecture in the interpretations of that "more sure word of prophecy" to which we are admonished to "take heed, as unto a light which shineth in a dark place." The fair inference is, that Origen, as the originator of the allegorical theory of interpretation, as Johann Lorenz von Mosheim (1693–1755) declares, "by an unhappy method, opened a secure retreat for all sorts of errors which a wild and irregular imagination could bring forth;" and that, as Joseph Milner (1744–1797) says, "no man, not altogether unsound and hypocritical, ever injured the Church more than Origen did;" and that hence, in the words of Luther, "the allegorical sense is commonly uncertain, and by no means safe to build upon; for as much as it usually depends on human opinion and conjecture only, on which, if a man lean, he will find it no better than an Egyptian reed."

And hence, having exposed the fallacy of the various theories which, as built upon Origen's "unhappy method" of interpreting "the teachings of Isaiah and John concerning the second coming of Christ," allege that they were all fulfilled, either first, by the return of the Jews from the Babylonish captivity; or second, by the overthrow of paganism and the establishment of Christianity in the Roman Empire under Constantine the Great in A.D. 325, as founded upon Revelation 20:1–7; or third, that the second coming of Christ was verified by the judgments inflicted upon the Jewish nation and government by the Roman army in A.D. 70, as founded upon our Lord's prophecy, Matthew 24:27–30; or finally fourth, as predicated of the Whitbyan (Daniel Whitby, 1638–1726) "New Hypothesis" of a spiritual coming of Christ, as founded upon Revelation 20:1–6; I repeat, having exposed the fallacy of these absolutely conflicting theories of "the Messianic prophecies," I proceed to lay before the reader a brief synopsis of the millenarian scheme of the second coming of Christ and of the millennial era, as taught in Holy Scripture, that he may have a more complete view of it as a whole.

Millenarianism teaches that the faith and hope of the Church, in every age, have been directed to and centered in the second personal coming of Christ, as that event which is to consummate her redemption from all physical and moral evil. (Hebrews 11:13–16; 35, 39, 40; 12:1, 2; 1 Corinthians 1:7; Philippians 3:20, 21; 2 Timothy 4:8; 2 Peter 3:12–14; Titus 1:1, 2; 2:1–13; 3:7; Romans 5:5; 8:24, 25; 15:13; Colossians 1:27; 2 Thessalonians 2:16; Hebrews 6:18, 19; 1 Peter 1:3; 1 John 3:3; Job 19:25–27; Isaiah 25:9; Matthew 16:27; 25:31–34; Mark 14:62; 1 Timothy 6:13, 14; Hebrews 9:27, 28; 1 Thessalonians 1:10; Romans 8:23; 1 Corinthians 1:7; 2 Thessalonians 3:5).

That the present Christian dispensation is that part of "the times of the Gentiles" called "the gospel of the kingdom," or the kingdom of God in "mystery," during which the gospel is to be preached to all nations as "a witness" of the truth, "to take out of (or from among) the Gentiles a people for Christ's name," as preparatory to their admission to "the kingdom of God" in manifestation. (Luke 21:24; Romans 11:25; Matthew 28:11; 24:14; Mark 4:11; Luke 8:10; Romans 16:25, 26; Ephesians 3:3, 4, 9; 1 Timothy 4:16; Revelation 10:7; Acts 15:14; Matthew 28:18–20; Mark 16:15, 16, 17–20; 1 Peter 1:1–9; 2 Timothy 4:6–8; Matthew 25:31–34).

We are now living toward that close of "the times of the Gentiles" called "the time of the end," Daniel 12:9—that is, not the end of time, but of the "world," the present age or dispensation. And henceforth, that as, by the acknowledgment of the whole Church, the second coming of Christ is to take place at the end of "the times of the Gentiles," we are now occupying a position proximate to that event. (Daniel 2:35, and verse 44; 7:11, 12, and verses 13, 14; 2 Thessalonians 2:3, 4, and verse 8). Accordingly, that there is no ground for the popular expectation of a millennium of universal righteousness, prosperity, and peace, as alleged to be effected by the conversion of all nations to Christ through ordinary church activities before His second coming. So far from it, that event is to be immediately preceded by the following ominous signs:

1. A prevalent ignorance of divine things among all classes. (Isaiah 60:2; Daniel 12:10; Isaiah 32:6, 7; Hosea 14:9; Romans 11:8–10; 2 Thessalonians 2:10–12; Revelation 9:20, 21).

2. A general apostasy from that "faith once delivered to the saints," and especially in the article of the Lord's

second coming. (Luke 18:8; 2 Thessalonians 2:1–3; 2 Peter 3:1–4).

3. A state of religious formalism, abounding iniquity, national and political revolutions, tyranny, anarchy, war, infidelity, and blasphemy. (Matthew 24:12; James 5:1–6; 1 Timothy 4:1–3; 2 Timothy 3:1–7; Isaiah 2:10–22; 5:26–30; 24:1–20; Jeremiah 25:15–29; Ezekiel 21:24–27; Haggai 2:7; Luke 21:7–11, and verses 25, 26; Daniel 7:8, 11, 20, 25; 2 Peter 1:12–15; Jude 10, 17–19; Revelation 13:1, 5, 6).

4. Nevertheless, in the midst of these general commotions in church and state, the gospel will accomplish its second circuit through the earth, when its work as a witness to the nations will end. (See Matthew 28:19; Mark 16:15. Then compare Romans 10:18, and Colossians 1:6, with Matthew 24:14, and Christ's promise, Matthew 28:20, which extends down to the end of the world—i.e., age or dispensation).

5. That there will also be an extensive spirit of inquiry among the true followers of Christ on the subject of His second coming. (Daniel 4:4, 9; Habakkuk 2:1–3; Matthew 25:6, 7).

6. That these "signs" will be attended with numerous corresponding physical phenomena in the earth and the heavens. (Micah 7:15, 16; Luke 21:25, 26. See also verse 11; and Revelation 16:18.)

7. That there will be an unprecedented manifestation of the power and malice of the Devil, in exciting the worst passions of national rulers and their subjects to acts of mutual violence, and of blasphemy against God. (Revelation 12:12; 13:4–8; followed by the effects, as symbolized in

Revelation 16:13, 14. See also Psalm 2:2, 3; and Revelation 16:9–11; 21).

8. That while there will be a waning of the temporal power of the Popedom, the spiritual superstition of the Papacy will revive and become dominant throughout Christendom, down to the close of "the times of the Gentiles," when it will be totally exterminated by the very power which has so long promoted and upheld it. (Compare Daniel 7:12, particularly the last clause, with Revelation 17:12, 15; and verses 16–18; taken in connection with chapter 17:1–21; 22–24).

9. That the same will apply to the wasting and decay of the Turco-Mohammedan Impostor, the total extinction of which, as the only impediment to the restoration of the Jews to Palestine, will be contemporaneous with the destruction of the Papal power. (Compare Daniel 8:8–12, and verses 21, 22; 23–25; with Revelation 9:14, and 16:12).

10. But, notwithstanding the marked character and significance of these "signs" as the immediate harbingers of the Lord's second coming, that the nominal church and the world, heedless of their prefigurative warnings, will be involved in a state of unemotional indifference, carnal self-security, and sensual indulgences. (Matthew 24:37–39; 1 Thessalonians 5:1–3; 2 Thessalonians 1:4–9; Revelation 18:7, 8).

Now, these last Scriptural references undeniably connect Christ's second coming with the moral and physical phenomena as indicated above, and hence demonstrate the impossibility that a millennium of universal righteousness and peace is to precede that event. The 8th and 9th of the above "signs," taken in connection with the others, when viewed in their relation to the second coming of Christ, prove impossible to refute that that event is "pre" and not post-millennial. In other words, inasmuch as the final destruction of the Papal and Turco-Mohammedan powers is to take place at the close of "the times of the Gentiles;" and this being, by the admission of the whole Christian Church, the time of the second coming of Christ; it follows, that no millennial kingdom or other power can come in between their destruction and that event. (First, of the Papal power, compare Daniel 7:11, 12, with verses 13, 14; also 20, 21, with verse 22; also verses 24, 25, with verses 26, 27. Second, of the Turco-Mohammedan power compare Daniel 8:9, 14, 23, with verse 25, last clause).

While "of that day and hour knoweth no man, not the angels in heaven, neither the Son, but the Father only" (Matthew 24:36), yet that prophecy reveals the proximate period when it will take place. All the "signs" enumerated above, and especially the 8th and 9th, are designed to indicate its near approach. Furthermore, it teaches that the great event that is to immediately accompany the second personal coming of Christ, is, the resurrection of those who sleep in Him, and the change and translation of those living saints who will remain until His coming, according to 1 Thessalonians 1:13–18; 1 Corinthians 15: 23; and which is called "the first resurrection," Revelation 20:5, 6. Also, that this coming of Christ in the first instance will be, not openly or visibly to all the world, but as it were secretly, like "a thief in the night," to steal away His waiting and watching saints, when "two shall be in one bed, the one shall be taken and the other left," (Matthew 24:43; Luke 12:39; 1 Thessalonians 5:2; 2 Peter 2:10; Revelation 16:15;

Luke 17:34–36).

CHAPTER 7

Structure of the Millennial Hierarchy

Similar to other earthly kingdoms, the Millennial Kingdom must have its King, its officers of state, its subjects,
and a territorial domain. It was in innocence "The earth and
the fullness thereof," created by the self-manifested "God
of Christ" as the territorial domain of his kingdom, and
of which "they that dwell therein," viewed representatively
in their federal head, were the subjects, were "the Lord's"
by rightful possession and sovereign rule. The "dominion"
given to man in Eden, was not a dominion over his own
kind. And, as his sin was an act of treason and rebellion
against his only rightful sovereign, the Christ of God, and
he was delivered over as a vassal to the Satanic usurper of
his Lordly rule down to the time of the predicted "restitution of all things;" when restored from the ruins of the
fall, it will consist of his recovery to and acknowledgment
of his allegiance to the only rightful King, the "woman's
Seed," Christ. Or, as in the instance of Israel's retraction of
the Theocracy in the time of Samuel, when God Himself
was their king; having "abode many days," "without a king,

or a prince, or a sacrifice, or an image," when they shall "afterward seek the Lord their God in the latter days," that Theocracy shall be restored to them under the reign of David's royal son, "The Prince of Peace." In accordance with God's covenant promise to Israel when restored to their own land—"I will restore thy judges as at the first, and thy counselors as at the beginning."; and again, "I will make thy officers peace, and thy exactors righteousness;" and also that, in matters of "controversy, the priests, the Levites, the sons of Zadok, shall stand in judgment," it is evident that they shall be invested with governmental powers. As with Israel of old, they will be comprised of a church and state union, with a ritual form of worship, and a corresponding system of government for the regulation of their civil, social, judicial, and religious affairs.

But I now add, that when "the first dominion shall come to the daughter of Zion, and the kingdom to the daughter of Jerusalem," as above, it will constitute the lowest, inasmuch as it will be the subordinate form of Government, under the restored theocracy of Israel. I now observe, therefore, that in the organic arrangement of the Millennial Hierarchy, the son of David, the Lord Jesus Christ, who is to sit upon his throne, is the Divinely appointed King, or head, around which, as the source of all authority, and the Center of Unity, all the lesser orders, like the planets around the sun, will revolve. (First, compare Psalm 89:4, 5, with Acts 2:29–35. See also Psalm 90; Matthew 22:42–45; 1 Corinthians 15:25; Ephesians 1:22; Hebrews 1:13. Second, 2 Samuel 7:12–16; Psalm 2:6–12; Isaiah 9:6, 7; Jeremiah 3:17; 33:17, 20, 21; Ezekiel 34:23, 24; 37:24, 25; Zechariah 14:9; Luke 1:31–33; 1 Corinthians 15:25; Hebrews 2:6–8).

All the nations of the earth, Jewish and Gentile, shall be subjected to His Divine Authority. (Daniel 2:44, 45; 7:13, 14; 22, 26, 27; Isaiah 32:1, 17, 18; Psalm 71:8–19; Micah 4:1–7; Zechariah 9:10; Revelation 11:15–18).

The raised and translated living saints share with Christ in the government of the nations of earth. (Psalm 47:3; 49:14; Isaiah 32:1; Daniel 7:21, 22; Matthew 19:28; Luke 19:17, 19; 22:29, 30; 1 Corinthians 4:4, 5; 6:2, 3; 9:25; 2 Timothy 4:8; 1 Peter 5:4; Revelation 1:6; 2:10, 26, 27; 3:21; 5:10; 20:4, 5, last clause, and verses 6, 7).

It is important to observe that many writers on this subject, by confounding things which differ, have indiscriminately combined those of the mortal with the immortal or resurrected state, as equally and in the same sense the occupants of the millennial new earth— which circumstance, more than any other, has subjected millenarians to the imputation of Judaizing and carnalizing the future state of Christ and His glorified saints. It becomes necessary to point out the distinct prophetic relation that will exist between the saved nations in the flesh, and Christ and His co-reigning saints, during the millennial era will involve an exhibit of the territorial domain assigned to the newly erected millennial kingdom of Christ. As this "kingdom" is said to be "under the whole heaven," Daniel 7:27, of course it must be on this earth. (Compare Isaiah 9:6, 7, with Psalm 22:28; and 67:4; 2:8; 82:8; Revelation 3:21; 5:10; 20:4, 6).

This refers to the earth, as renewed or regenerated by "fire" at the last day, i.e., the seventh millenary of the world, in the morning of which it will be partial only, preparing it for the millennial "new heavens and earth" state predicted by Isaiah, chapter 65, (compare verse 17, with 18, 19; and chapter 66, compare verse 22 with 23, 24). See also Ezekiel 38:18–23; 39:6. But in the evening of that day, it will be total, corresponding with the state of the "new heavens and new earth" of Peter and John. (Compare 2 Peter 3:8, with verses 9–12, and 13; and Revelation 21:1–5, and chapter 20:9). This will prepare it for the eternal abode of the redeemed.

The distinction between these two states of the renewed earth will appear from the following comparison. The former will not be totally exempt from existing evil, sin, and death, (See Isaiah 65:20, and 66:23, 24. See Revelation 20:1, 4; 22:3–5; 11, 15).

For the metropolis of the millennial earth, see Isaiah 2:2–4; 24:23; 60:8–14; Joel 3:16, 17, 20; Zechariah 14:17–21; Ezekiel 42:7. Reference is made here to the ancient city of Jerusalem when rebuilt. It is to be located in the "holy oblation [offering] or portion," upon the division of the land, on the north next to Judah, (Ezekiel 45:1–3; 48:7, 8; 30, 31). In this city is to be erected the new "sanctuary" or temple, (Ezekiel 45:3; 48:21). And also a "tabernacle," (Ezekiel 37:25–27).

But there is to be a second city, Ezekiel 48:15. This "city" is located in the "holy portion" on the south, next to Benjamin, whose "border," like that of Judah, extends from east to west, (verse 23).

Then there is to be a third city, called "the Holy City, New Jerusalem," (Revelation 21:2, 10). In this "city" there is also to be a "tabernacle," (Revelation 21:3). And finally, both Ezekiel and John speak of a new river, whose borders on either side will be lined with fruit-bearing trees. (Compare Ezekiel 47:12, with Revelation 22:2).

Now, a perusal of the above references will show, that

these three cities, together with the sanctuary, or temple, and tabernacle, and the river of Ezekiel and of the Apocalypse, are totally separate and distinct each from the other as it concerns their respective localities, their uses, and the order of time in which they are to appear. As it is perfectly apparent that the "heavens and earth" state of Isaiah, chapter 65 and 66, is pre-millennial, and that of Peter and John, 2 Peter 3, and Revelation 21:1, 5, is post-millennial, with the period of a thousand years intervening. So, the first two cities, together with the sanctuary or temple, the tabernacle, and the new river of Ezekiel, belong to the millennial new earth state: while the third city, and the tabernacle and new river of John, belong to the eternal new earth state.

But, from the time that Messiah visibly appears to Israel, when they shall exclaim, "Lo, this is our God, we have waited for Him, and He will save us: this is the Lord, we have waited for Him, we will be glad and rejoice in His salvation" (Isaiah 25:9), the prophets declare that "Jerusalem shall be called the throne of the Lord" (Jeremiah 2:17), and that he will "dwell in the midst of them," (Zephaniah 3:14, 15; Zechariah 2:10–12; and 8:3; Psalm 135:21; and Isaiah 24:23). Also, that "the name of the city from that day shall be, the Lord is there" (Ezekiel 48:35). And again, that both Ezekiel and John declare that His "Sanctuary shall be in the midst of them," and His Tabernacle shall be with men," (Ezekiel 37:25–27; Revelation 21:3). And finally, as of the saints it is declared that they shall be "kings and priests unto God and the Lamb," so they are to "sit with Him in His Throne," and "reign on the earth," (Revelation 3:12; and verse 21; also chapter 5:10; 20:4).

Now, many expositors having confounded the "new

heavens and earth" states of Isaiah, Peter, and John, insisting that they are identical; have also, first, confounded the two cities of Ezekiel with the Holy City or New Jerusalem of John. Second, the same with the tabernacles of Ezekiel and John, insisting that they are identical with the New Jerusalem of the latter prophet. And then, third, alleging that "the holy city, or new Jerusalem" of the Apocalypse, will be the abode of Christ, and his co-reigning saints during the millennial era. From the above descriptions of their presence in the Jerusalem and second city of Ezekiel, they insist, fourth, that all the above-named phrases refer to one and the same thing, as denoting that the future inheritance of the raised and changed saints during the millennial era, is identical with that of the occupants of the earth in the flesh.

Now if this is so, it renders the millenarian scheme justly obnoxious to the charge, that it is a Judaizing and carnalizing future state and condition of Christ and His glorified saints. But, a careful discrimination between things which differ, as connected with the several cities spoken of, their occupants, the relations of rulers and the ruled as predicated of the organic structure of the millennial hierarchy, and the distinction to be drawn between the millennial and the eternal state portrayed in the above prophecies, will sufficiently give evidence to the fallacy of the above theories, and with it the injustice of the imputation against the millenarian scheme.

To this end, it is only necessary to take into account: 1. The distinction drawn between the millennial new heavens and earth state of Isaiah, and that of Peter and John, after an intervening period of a thousand years. 2.

That the two cities, together with the sanctuary and the tabernacle of Ezekiel, pertain to the millennial state of the renewed earth. 3. That the two cities, together with the sanctuary and tabernacle, located in the holy oblation or portion of Ezekiel, form the metropolis of the millennial earth state, occupied by the saved nations in the flesh. 4. Between these, as the subjects of the millennial kingdom, and the Lord Jesus Christ as their king, together with his coordinate immortal and glorified saints, there will be kept up a continued communication from His seat or throne "in the air" (See 1 Thessalonians 4:17), as the capital of His universal earthly empire, onward to the period of "the end, when He will deliver up" the millennial "kingdom to God, even the Father...that God may be all in all." (1 Corinthians 15:24–28).

It therefore follows, that there is a wide distinction in the prophetic writings, between the respective relations and spheres of action of the living races of men, and of the risen and glorified redeemed Church of Christ. The former are of the lineal multitudinous seed of Abraham, and of the Gentile nations gathered unto them, during the millennial era. The latter, in virtue of their prior faith in Christ, who is emphatically the "seed" of Abraham, and who are of the "Jerusalem that is above," have a union with Zion's King that is not of an earthly, but of a heavenly origin, and are therefore of the "election" according to grace, whether they are Jews or Gentiles by nature, all being one in Christ Jesus; so that, when they are gathered into one "at the appearing of Christ," on the morning of "the first resurrection," they will constitute the mystical body of the glorious Head—His spouse—His Bride, whose high destiny is, not to be ruled over, but to rule, as kings and priests unto God. The scriptural meaning of the word "inheritance," in its application to the two classes of the literal and spiritual seed of Abraham, will afford additional light on this important subject. Apply it, first, to the literal Israel as the Lord's inheritance. (Deuteronomy 32:8, 9; Psalm 135:4). Second, to the land of Canaan as their inheritance, in connection with the Gentile strangers among them, (Ezekiel 47:13, 14; 22, 23). And on the other hand, first, Christ has a glorious inheritance in His Saints. (Compare Ephesians 5:27, with chapter 1:18, and verses 15–23 inclusive). This will be revealed when He appears the second time. (Compare Hebrews 9:28, with 2 Thessalonians 1:10). Second, the saints also have an inheritance in Christ. (See Ephesians 1:11–14).

Now, this "inheritance," for which the saints of the "first resurrection" have an earnest or title deed in Christ, is entirely separate and distinct from that of the Jewish and Gentile saved nations in the flesh. It is typified by that which the priests and Levites had in God under the law, as occupying the place and enjoying the privileges of the first-born, as the Lord spoke unto Moses, (Numbers 3:12, 13; and Deuteronomy 18:1, 2; and also by Ezekiel, chapter 44:28). With these passages, compare James 1:18; Revelation 14:4; Hebrews 12:23. In the enrolling of names in this last passage, allusion is made to the numbering and recording the names of the first-born among the Israelites, (Numbers 3, and chapter 8; and, as such, they are said to be "redeemed from the earth," Revelation 14:3, i.e., in resurrection glory, Romans 8:23, and thereafter belong to Christ as his "jewels," Malachi 3:17, and shall be admitted to that "inheritance incorruptible, undefiled, and that fadeth not away," 1 Peter 1:3, 4, which, now "reserved in heaven for them," shall be "revealed in the last time...at the appearing of Christ," verses 4, 5, 7.

It is therefore evident, that the elect saints—the Church of the First-born—as the espoused Bride of the Lamb, never will have an abiding inheritance upon the restored Paradisical "new earth" of Isaiah during the millennial era. The reason is obvious. Those in mortal flesh, whose "inheritance" is on the earth, as we have seen, being of the natural seed of Abraham, are to some extent subject to both sin and death. Whereas the saints of the resurrection, being "heirs of God, and joint-heirs with Christ," who is the divinely constituted "heir of all things," will be exalted to resurrection life "in the air to be ever with Him."

And now, as to the mode of communication to be kept up between Christ as Zion's King in conjunction with the "first born" of the resurrection as His "kings and priests," and the saved nations in the flesh. Though our knowledge of it is limited, still, with the ladder in Jacob's vision present in our minds, with its foot resting on earth and its top reaching to heaven, and the Lord standing above it, while the angels of God were seen ascending and descending upon it (Genesis 28:10–13), we may consider ourselves as furnished with some useful suggestions in explanation of this subject; and especially when we take into account the numerous statements already given of Christ's personal presence with His people on earth during the millennial era, and of the statement regarding the resurrected saints, that they will be "equal unto the angels," i,e., in wisdom, and in the powers of locomotion, by which they will be qualified to descend from and ascend to their aerial thrones (See Revelation 20:4), in the execution of the commands of Zion's King, among the millennial inhabitants of earth. Why, did not Jesus, in His resurrected and glorified humanity, appear among, and eat and drink with, His disciples? And when He arose, did not many of the saints who slept arise with Him and enter into the Holy City and appear to many? And has the earth not often been trodden by angels' feet? And do we not find that everywhere in the universe of God there are ranks and degrees? Among the angels there is an hierarchy. And also, "in the resurrection" state, one star will differ from another star in glory." In the world to come, therefore, there will be those who rule, and those who are ruled; Jesus Christ, seated upon His father David's throne, swaying His righteous scepter over all; "the apostles, sitting on twelve thrones, judging the twelve tribes of Israel;" and the resurrected saints, also enthroned; and which, taken together, will constitute that glorious millennial hierarchy or theocracy of the world to come, of which we speak.

And finally, on this subject of the communication between Christ and His saints with the occupants of the millennial earth. It is not necessary, in order to meet the requirements of the prophecies in reference to it, that it should be uninterrupted. It may be illustrated by the condition of our blessed Lord, during the forty days' interval between His resurrection and ascension. He had then no fixed habitation, nor did He associate with men as He was accustomed to do before His crucifixion. It was seldom that He showed Himself even to His own disciples, and all His appearances were miraculous. They did not know where He came, nor where He went. It might be in a room, where the doors were closed, that He suddenly stood in the midst of them, they not perceiving how He obtained admittance. Or it might be on the public highway, or in the open fields, or by the seaside, that He joined their circle and their conversation. But in every case they were taught that their risen Lord's resurrected human body had acquired superhuman or supernatural power of concealment or of manifestation. As such, we are warranted to expect that the saints, when raised in their spiritualized bodies, and made like Him, shall also possess this extraordinary power as above intimated, of appearing and disappearing at will.

To conclude: The two cities of Ezekiel, though possessing several marks of resemblance (compare Ezekiel 48:31–34, with Revelation 21:12, 13), yet, besides other points of dissimilarity, while the former are to be located within the bounds of the "Holy Oblation [offering]," John saw the latter "descending from God out of heaven," Revelation 21:2, 10. Besides, this follows, in the order of time, the creation of the post-millennial "new heavens and earth" by the "fire" of the last conflagration. (Compare 2 Peter 2:7–13, with Revelation 21:1, 5).

This stands connected with the closing scene of time— the last Gog and Magog apostasy—their attempted assault upon "the camp of the saints and the beloved city"— their destruction by "fire from God out of heaven"— the resurrection of the wicked dead when the millennial thousand years are "finished"—the assemblage of "the dead small and great" before "the great white throne"— their trial and condemnation, which have so long awaited them, even unto this "the day of judgment and perdition of ungodly men," when "death and hell shall be cast into the lake of fire, which is the second death;" and when "whosoever shall not be found written in the book of life, shall be cast into the lake of fire." Then will follow, the great voice from heaven, saying "Behold, the tabernacle of God is with men, and he will dwell with them, and they shall be His people, and God himself shall be with them, and be their God. And God shall wipe away all tears from their eyes; and there shall be no more death, neither sorrow nor crying, neither shall there be any more pain: for the former things are passed away."

This is that eternal state in the "new heavens and a new earth wherein dwelleth righteousness."

PART TWO

History of Millennialism

I t is maintained, in the sequel to "Our Bible Chronology," and also in this reply to Dr. Shedd's (William Greenough Thayer Shedd, 1820–1894) chapter on "Eschatology," that, independently of the details of Scripture chronology, historic and prophetic, God has revealed in His word the precise period of 6,000 years (which that chronology will be found exactly to fill up to a year), between the creation and fall, and the Christian dispensation, as that within which all His ordinary purposes of providence and grace toward mankind were to be accomplished, and which is to be immediately followed by the seventh millenary of rest, in exact analogy to the six days of formation of the earth and heavens, and the seventh day of the Divine Sabbatic repose.

But in determining the commencing period, and the closing period of the seventh millenary of the world, we must repair to the historic and prophetic chronology of Scripture. There is, however, a variation between the Hebrew and the Greek Septuagint chronologies. There are also variations in the computations of both by different chronographers. The first point to be settled, therefore, is, which of the two, the original Hebrew or the Greek Septuagint is authoritative in determining the true chronology of the world's history from the creation and fall of man. We adopt the Hebrew as our standard. And, as to the Hebrew chronology for the nativity, we have demonstrated the true date to be 4132 years, instead of 4,004, as that adopted in our common version from Archbishop Usher. The difference between the Hebrew chronology and that of the Septuagint, stands as such: To the Nativity, according to the corrected Hebrew, 4,132 years. To the Nativity, according to the Septuagint, 5,871 years. This gives an excess of the Septuagint over the Hebrew of 1,739 years.

The important connection which the chronology of Scripture holds in settling the question of the commencement and close of the seventh "chiliad," is our apology for introducing it in this place. Some of the ancient writers, as Augustine and others, and some of modern times, as Grotius, and Prideaux, adhere to the chronology of the Septuagint, which circumstance (as no two of them agree in their computations) accounts for their commencing what they call the millennium, from so many different stand points.

With these remarks premised, we would respectfully commend to the special notice of the author of the *History of Christian Doctrine* (Dr. Shedd) what we deferentially claim as a demonstration, that the ideas and language of the New Testament writers in reference to the second personal coming of Christ and the judgment of the great day, were all derived from and founded upon the prophetic statements of the inspired pre-Christian-Jewish writers regarding them; e.g., Isaiah, Jeremiah, Ezekiel, and especially the prophet Daniel.

ANCIENT MILLENARIANISM

Now, Professor Shedd admits that "the Jews, at the time of the incarnation, were expecting a personal prince, and a corporeal reign, in the Messiah who was to come. We, of course, here take it for granted that the Professor speaks, of the Jewish nation, as it was, when Christ appeared among them. The question, therefore, is, on what was their expectation founded? What but the following and similar prophecies, too numerous to quote in this place? First, in reference to their restoration: "Thus saith the Lord God, I will even gather you from the people, and assemble you out of the captivities where ye have been scattered, and I will give you the land of Israel." Second, the dominion and kingdom that was to be restored to them: "And thou, O tower of the flock, the strong hold of the daughter of Zion, unto thee shall it come, even the first dominion; the kingdom shall come to the daughter of Zion." Third, the King who should reign over them: "Behold, the days come, saith the Lord, that I will raise unto David a righteous Branch (Messiah), and a King shall reign and prosper; and shall execute judgment and justice in the earth." And again: "The Lord shall reign in mount Zion, and in Jerusalem, and before His ancients gloriously." Then too, fourth, all the Gentile nations were to be gathered to restored Judah: "And the Gentiles shall come to thy light, and kings to the brightness of thy rising."

These examples must suffice. The "later Jews," in Christ's time, interpreted these prophecies literally. Hence our account of the origin of millenarianism. We repeat: it antedated, by thousands of years, the time of these "later Jews." It reaches back to the first promise of redemption by Christ, which promise was renewed in the covenant of God with Abraham and his seed, through whom all the families and kindreds of the Gentiles were to be blessed, and of whom "Christ is the minister of the circumcision for the truth of God, to confirm the promises made unto the fathers."

Thus much, then, as to the source whereby these "later Jews" derived their expectation of "a personal prince, and a corporeal reign, in the Messiah which was to come." What does the Professor think of it?

But this is not all. The belief that the earth, and the moral and religious state of its inhabitants, were to undergo a great change at the end 6,000 years, has been detected in the traditionary writings of the Pagan nations. On this subject, Bishop Russell, of Scotland, though an anti-millenarian, says: "With respect to the millennium, it must be acknowledged that the doctrine concerning it stretches back into antiquity so remote and obscure, that it is impossible to fix its origin." Not quite, Doctor. Let us see what may be gathered.

From Pagan writers. The Chaldeans, according to Plutarch, believed in a struggle between good and evil for a space of 6,000 years, "and then Hades is to cease, and men are to be happy, neither wanting food nor making shade." True, Plutarch assigns no reasons for their belief; but it was, without doubt, like all their other notions regarding the origin of all things, derived by tradition from the inspired patriarchal writings. The learned Mr. George Stanley Faber affirms it to have been the doctrine also of the Persians and Etruscans, particularly the latter, who taught that the world was formed in the course of six periods, each period forming a millenary; while 6,000 years is allotted to a seventh period, i.e., that of its duration. "Zoroaster, an ancient Persian philosopher, the author of the Zendavesta, or Persian Bible, and the founder of the Magians, also taught the same thing. Dr. Prideaux supposes him to have been a contemporary of the prophet Daniel, from whom, as also from the other Hebrew prophets, Dr. Hengstenberg thinks he stole and adulterated the truths of revelation. He taught that in "the last times," after much evil of every kind had afflicted the earth, two beings of supernatural powers would appear and extensively restore mankind. In the end another superior personage, viz., Sociach—a name resembling in sound the Hebrew word Messiah—would make his appearance, under whose reign the dead would be raised, the judgment take place, and the earth renovated and glorified. And finally, a still superior righteous judge, Ormuzd, from an elevated place, commands Sociach to render to all men their deserts, and take the pure to his own presence. He also taught the six-millennial duration of the earth. Bishop Russell also states, that Theopompus, who flourished 340 years B.C., relates that the Persian magi taught that the present state of things would continue 6,000 years, after which Hades, the place and state of departed spirits, would be destroyed, and that mankind would then live happily. But, from these pre-Christian-Jewish and Pagan writers, let us now turn to those of the Christian church, and of the apostolic age.

On this subject, as we have already seen, Professor Shedd makes the following statement: "The disciples of Christ, being themselves Jews, were at first naturally affected with these [millenarian] views." But that after the day of Pentecost, they rose above their early Jewish education and that "in none of their inspired writings do we find such an expectation."

We must here premise, in the first place, that our blessed Lord himself, when predicting the restoration of Israel at the close of the "times of the Gentiles" (Luke 21:24), directs them to "look up and lift up their heads at their approaching redemption," when they shall see the "signs" immediately preceding His "coming in a cloud," "begin to come to pass." (Luke 21:27, 28). Or, if He alludes to the millennial kingdom which the God of heaven shall set up at the destruction of the anti- Christian nations (Daniel 2:34, 35; compare verses 44, 45), when "the kingdom, and dominion, and greatness of the kingdom under the whole heaven shall be given to the saints of the Most High (Daniel 7:13, 14, 27), still this "kingdom of God is nigh at hand," only when the indications of His return are observable, (Luke 21:27–31). Or, if to correct a misapprehension on the part of his "disciples," as though "the kingdom of God was then nigh at hand," He rehearses to them the parable of the "nobleman, who went into a far country, to receive a kingdom and to return," (Luke 19:11–27); the obvious purport of it was, to teach them that in the case of a nobleman going into a far country, entrusting his servants with money, that they may testify their love to him by a right use of his property in the interval, and returning after he has received a kingdom, to reward the obedient and punish those wicked "citizens" who had driven him into exile; I repeat: the obvious purport of it was, to suggest to them the idea of subsequent continued residence, which ill comports with the popularly received view of Christ's returning merely for the purpose of pronouncing sentence upon all at the close of the millennium.

Now then we appeal,—in view of these teachings of Christ himself—all of which are in perfect harmony with what "Moses in the law, and David in the Psalms, and all the prophets wrote concerning Him"—can it be believed that "the disciples of Christ," because they were "Jews," were "naturally infected with these views, " only on the ground that it was the "doctrine" taught by the "later-Jewish" nation in Christ's time? More than all: is it to be credited that those glorious things which all the older prophets have announced concerning the future redemption of Israel and Judah, and of which prophets have sung in strains of highest rapture—which sustained them in the hour of their fiery trial to picture imagery which cheered them during their long and weary pilgrimage, and enabled them to "die in faith" of those promises which they "beheld afar off," together with the above prophetic utterances of our blessed Lord. Is it to be credited that "none of the inspired writings" of the apostles treat the doctrine of the second personal coming of our Lord in accordance with those teachings. If such predictions really contain allusions to the millennium, so also are they intimately connected with the Savior's return, and resurrection of his saints. But if these do not contain allusions to the millennium, then are there no references to it in either the Gospels or Epistles? But, so far from this, the only difficulty arises from not knowing where to begin the citations. We must confine ourselves mostly to the epistolary writings.

First, then, in the exercise of their faith in the return of that Master for whom they took joyfully the spoiling of their goods, and in testimony to whose Messiahship they cheerfully laid down their lives, that they fully believed in the realization of the Church's hopes, to be accomplished only by the establishment of the predicted "kingdom," Peter declared concerning Christ, "whom the heavens must receive, until the times of restitution of all things, which God hath spoken by the mouth of all his holy prophets since the world began." (Acts 3:21). And in harmony with this, Paul declares that unto them was "made known the mystery of God's will according to his good pleasure, which he hath purposed in himself, that in the dispensation of the fullness of times, he might gather together in one all things in Christ, both which are in heaven and which are on earth." (Ephesians 1:9, 10). And further, as to the process of this: First, a large portion of the eleventh chapter of the Romans is devoted by the apostle to demonstrating the final restoration and conversion of the remnant of Israel according to the election of grace, when "the Deliverer shall come to Zion, and shall turn away ungodliness from Jacob:" for then, "all Israel shall be saved." And Peter, speaking of the Gentile believers, says: "And when the Chief Shepherd shall appear, they shall receive a crown of glory that fadeth not away." (1 Peter 5:4). And this shall be, says Paul, "when the Lord himself shall descend from heaven with a shout, with the voice of the archangel, and with the trump of God; and the dead in Christ shall rise first," while they "which are alive and remain unto the coming of the Lord, shall be caught up to meet the Lord in the air, and so shall ever be with the Lord." (1 Thessalonians 4:13–17). Then also, in reference to the millennial "new heavens and new earth" predicted by Isaiah, when the Lord will "create Jerusalem a rejoicing and her people a joy" (Isaiah 55:17,

18, and 66:20–22). Paul speaks of the removal from the inferior creation of the burden that they have been made to endure, in immediate connection with "the adoption," or "redemption of our body," at "the manifestation of the sons of God." (Romans 8:19–23). And again: when Paul speaks of the destruction of the Man of Sin, which shall immediately precede the millennium, he asserts that "him shall the Lord destroy with the brightness of His coming." (2 Thessalonians 2:8). So also, in treating of that "rest which remaineth for the people of God" (Hebrews 4:9), he refers to that seventh millenary in "the world to come" (habitable earth to come) (Hebrews 2:5), during which, as John declares, Satan shall be bound and the saints shall reign with Christ a thousand years." (Revelation 20:1–3, 4–6). And yet, according to Professor Shedd, "in none of their inspired writings do we find such an expectation" of Christ's second coming and kingdom on earth, as that spoken of by the old prophetic seers and by Christ himself! But we now pass on, to introduce in this place what may be gleaned from the ancient Jewish uninspired writers on this subject.

Speaking of these, Bishop Russell says there is "no room for doubt that the notion of a millennium preceded by several centuries the introduction of the Christian faith." Rabbi Elias, a Jewish doctor of high celebrity, whose opinion is called by the Jews "a tradition of the house of Elias," and who flourished about 200 years before Christ, taught that the world would be "2000 years void of the law; 2,000 years under the law; and 2,000 years under the Messiah." He limited the duration of the world to 6,000 years, and held that in the seventh millenary, "the earth would be renewed and the righteous dead raised; that these should not again be turned to dust, and that the just then alive should mount up with wings as the angels;" so that in that day they would not fear, though the mountains be cast into the midst of the sea." (Psalm 46:3). On this passage Bishop Russell observes, "that by this resurrection he meant a resurrection prior to the millennium is evident." Dr. Gregory also, a learned mathematician and astronomer in Oxford, England, who died in A. D. 1710, says: "In the first verse of the first chapter of Genesis, the Hebrew *Aleph*, which in the Jewish arithmetic stands for 1,000, is found six times. From this the ancient cabalists concluded that the world would last 6,000 years. Because also, God was six days about the creation, and a thousand years with Him are but as one day. (Psalm 90. See also 2 Peter 3:8). Therefore after six days, that is, 6,000 years duration of the world, there shall be a seventh day, or millenary sabbath of rest." Baal Katturim observes: "That at the end of 6,000 years the world shall return to its old state, without form and void, and after that, it shall wholly become a sabbath." The author also of Cespar Mishna, in his notes on Maimonides, writes: "At the end of 6,000 years will be the day of judgment, and it will also be a sabbath, the beginning of the world to come. The sabbath year, and year of jubilee, intend the same thing." And finally (though these quotations might be greatly extended): in the Gemarah, or comment on the Mishna, we read: "Rabbi Katina has said, that in the last of the thousands of years of the world's continuance, the world shall be destroyed; of which period it is said, 'the Lord alone shall be exalted in that day.'" (Isaiah 2:11). And tradition agrees with Rabbi Katina; for even as every seventh year is a year of release, so of the seventh thousand year of the world, it shall be a thousand years of release. We now resume the regular chain of history from the close of the New Testament age, by passing on to the early post-apostolic era.

EARLY POST APOSTOLIC

We observe that in addition to the tradition of the pre-Christian Jewish writers, that the six days of creation were designed to typically represent 6000 years, to be followed by a seventh millenary of rest and triumph over their enemies. The New Testament Scriptures also recognize the same principle of analogy of the one with the other. We ask: Was not the first Adam created as the figure of Christ the coming One? If then, we can go back to the fountain-head of time, and find a type of "the second man, the Lord from heaven," as He who by a second creation is to restore all things from the ruins of the fall; why should it be thought incredible, that the six days of formation of the material heavens and earth, and a seventh of rest, should bear a like character? Did not God create the world in six days, and rest on the seventh? Why did He not employ five, or ten, or twenty instead? And so, accordingly, Paul, Colossians 2:16, 17, alluding to the typical character of the preceding dispensation, speaks especially "in respect of the sabbath days"—of which, the seventh day of the Creator's repose from His six days' work was the first—and denominates them a "shadow of good things to come." Or, if this is thought to be an unwarrantable stretching of a type in regard to this first sabbath, we would direct the reader to Paul's use of the word "Sabbatism" in Hebrews 4:9, where, especially considering that it was Hebrew Christians whom he was addressing, and that, from long-continued usage, they could not do otherwise than associate it with a chronological septenary, he employed it to designate the saints' anticipated and ardently prayed-for season of glorious rest with Christ.

If, therefore, as is undeniable, the inspired apostle applied this seventh day or first sabbath of creative rest as a type of the heavenly rest to come, how can we consistently withhold from the previous six days of creative labor a similar typical character, as denotive of the 6,000 years that were to precede the seventh of rest? As "a shadow of good things to come," the apostle refers primarily to that millennial "rest which remaineth for the people of God" under the reign of Messiah and his saints, which is most explicitly declared to consist of "a thousand years;" while both David and Peter declare that "one day is with the Lord as a thousand years, and a thousand years as one day."

But, to the above may be added the fact, that the primitive fathers of that purest age of the Church immediately following the apostles, continued to put forth the same sentiment; and that, not as mere opinions based upon the uninspired pre Jewish-Christian traditions regarding it; but, with the additional light reflected upon it by the teachings of the New Testament writers as an article of Christian faith. In the quotations which follow, will be found a number of those early millenarian fathers, who spoke directly to the point under consideration. The first to be introduced to the reader's notice is Barnabas.

Of the Epistle still extant which bears his name, though Eusebius and Jerome pronounce it apocryphal, it is nevertheless esteemed genuine by such writers as Archbishops Wake and Usher, by Bishop Fell, and Drs. Mill,

Cave, Burnet, S. Clarke, and Mr. Whiston and others. In this Epistle (which doubtless Eusebius and Jerome wished to bring into disrepute on account of the millenarianism of its author), Barnabas, having argued that the Abrahamic covenant was perpetual, and that it had been fulfilled so far as it related to Christ's first coming in the flesh; from Isaiah 42:6 and 61:21, he exhibits Christ as the covenant pledge for the accomplishment of the remaining part of its stipulations at "the times of restitution of all things." He then goes on to say: "Furthermore it is written concerning the Sabbath, 'sanctify the sabbath of the Lord with pure hands and a clean heart.' And elsewhere he says, 'if thy children shall keep my sabbaths, then will I put my mercy on them' (alluding to the mercy promised to Abraham). And even in the beginning of the creation he makes mention of the Sabbath: 'And God made in six days the works of his hands, and finished them on the seventh day, and he rested on the seventh day and sanctified it'" And he then adds: "Consider, my children, what this signifies: 'He finished them in six days.' The meaning is this: that in 6,000 years the Lord will bring all things to an end. 'For with him one day is as a thousand years.' Therefore, children, in six days (i.e., 6,000 years) shall all things be accomplished. And what does he mean, and *rested on the seventh day?* He means that when His Son shall come, and abolish the wicked one, and judge the ungodly, and change the sun and moon and stars, that He shall gloriously rest on the seventh day. Behold, therefore, when we have received the righteous promise, when iniquity shall be no more, all things being renewed by the Lord, we shall be able to sanctify it, ourselves being holy. (Barnabas wrote in A.D. 71). He is supposed to have been martyred about A.D. 75, being stoned to death by the Jews.

Professor Shedd tells us that "there are no traces of chiliasm in the writings of Clement of Rome, Ignatius, Polycarp," but, let us see.

Clement of Rome in his first Epistle says: "Let us be followers of those who went about in goatskins and sheepskins, preaching the coming of Christ. Such were the prophets." Again, alluding to some who scoff at the apparent delay of Christ's second coming, he says: "Ye see how in a little while the fruit of the trees come to maturity. Of a truth, yet a little while, and His will shall be accomplished suddenly, the Holy Scripture itself bearing witness that He shall come quickly and not tarry; and the Lord shall suddenly come to his temple, even the Holy One whom ye look for." In his second Epistle he says: "If therefore we shall do what is just in the sight of God, we shall enter into his kingdom...Wherefore let us every hour expect the kingdom of God in love and righteousness, because we know not the day of God's appearing." Clement was martyred under the emperor Trajan about A.D. 100, by being thrown into the sea.

To the Ephesians Ignatius expresses his faith this way: "The last times are come upon us; let us therefore be very reverent and fear the long suffering of God, that it be not to us condemnation." To Polycarp he wrote: "Be every day better than another; consider the times, and expect Him who is above all time." Writing to the Smyrnians on the resurrection of Christ, He tells them that Peter and the other apostles did actually prove the same by the sense of touch, "being convinced both by the flesh and spirit." This belief, in connection with his hope of having a part in the first resurrection, was what led him to despise death and aspire after martyrdom, which was a general characteristic of the Christians of that age. Hence he expresses himself: "If I suffer, I shall then become the free man of Jesus Christ, and shall rise free." He was devoured by lions in the amphitheater of Rome in A.D. 107.

Dr. Burnet pronounces Polycarp a decided millenarian, and Eusebius hints the same. In his Epistle he taught that God had raised up our Lord Jesus Christ from the dead, and that he will come to judge the world and raise the saints, and that if we walk worthy of him we shall reign together with him. "Every one," he says, "that confesses not that Jesus Christ is come in the flesh, is antichrist...And whosoever shall say that there is neither resurrection nor judgment to come, that man is the first-born of Satan." Being a disciple of John, he must have received the doctrine directly from him. He was burned at the stake about A.D. 167.

The next in order comes Hermas. This early father, having predicted great tribulation as awaiting the Church, says: "Happy ye, as many as shall endure the great trial at hand." He also says: "This world is also as the winter to the righteous men, because they are not known, but dwell among sinners; but the world to come is a summer to them." Again he says: "The great God will remove the heavens, and the mountains, the hills and the seas: and the end will be accomplished that all things may be filled with His elect, who will possess the world to come."..."This age must be destroyed by fire, but in the age to come the elect of God shall dwell."

Papas, in the preface to his *Narratives of the Sayings of*

our Lord says that "he did not follow various opinions, but had the apostles for his authors; and that he considered what Andrew, what Peter, what Philip, what Thomas, and other disciples of the Lord said; as also what Aristian and John the senior, disciples of the Lord, what they spoke; and that He did not profit so much by reading books, as by the living voice of those persons which resounded from them." This is Jerome's account of Papias. Eusebius records his words: "Nor will you be sorry, that, together with our interpretations, I commit to writing those things which I have formerly learned from the elders and committed to memory. For I never (as many do) have followed those who abound in words, but rather those who taught the truth; not those who taught certain new and unaccustomed precepts, but those who remembered the commands of our Lord, handed down in parables, and proceeding from truth itself, i.e., the Lord. If I met with any one who had been conversant with the elders, from him I diligently inquired what were the sayings of the elders...The elders who had seen John, the disciple of our Lord, taught concerning those times (the millennium), and said, the 'days come, when the vine shall bring forth abundantly,...and all other fruits,...and all animals shall become peaceful and harmonious, one to the other, being perfectly obedient to man. But these things are credible only to those who have faith.' Then Judas, the betrayer, not believing, and asking how such fertility should be brought about, our Lord said, 'They shall see who come to those times.' And, of these very times Isaiah prophesying said, 'The wolf and the lamb shall dwell together.'" This is recorded by Papias as a discourse of our Lord, handed down by John the Evangelist. Eusebius himself speaks of

Papias: "Other things also, the same writer has set forth, as having come down to him by unwritten tradition, some new parables and discourses of our Savior. Among these, he says, that there will be a certain thousand years after the resurrection of the dead, when the kingdom of Christ will be established visibly in the earth." Papias here alludes to the seventh millenary after the 6000 years of the world's history. Eusebius affirms that "most of the ecclesiastical writers" believed with Papias; and Dr. Whitby admits that he taught concerning the millennium, that "it shall be a reign of Christ bodily on earth." While Dr. Burton allows that Papias' "proximity to the apostolic times, if not his personal acquaintance with some of the apostles, would put him in possession of many facts;" the learned Greswell observes that "Papias's honesty has never been impeached, and his antiquity makes his testimony to the millennium so much the more valuable."

Justin Martyr was a Greek, born at Annapolis or Sichem, in the province of Samaria, in Palestine, about A.D. 89. As a writer, he flourished between A.D. 148–165. He was therefore contemporary in part with Polycarp, Papias, and Irenaeus. Eusebius says his works stood in high credit among the early Christians. In his *Dialogue with Trypho, the Jew*, which is held to be authentic and genuine, having become a convert to "chiliasm" of a pure character, he looked for no millennium during this dispensation. He speaks of those as "destitute of just reason who did not understand that which is clear from all the Scriptures, that two comings of Christ were announced;" and he maintained that the millennium would be beyond the resurrection (i.e., of the saints), and in the restitution of all things, quoting Isaiah 65, and others of the prophets, as proof, especially verses 17–19, "Behold, I create new heavens and a new earth." And in reference to those in his time who denied this doctrine, in answer to the question of Trypho in regard to his faith, he says that, among other things, "I have demonstrated to thee that these are indeed called Christians, but are atheists and infamous heretics, because that in all things they teach what is blasphemous, ungodly, and unsound." We presume he here refers to the Gnostics of that age, whose system was a combination of Oriental and Platonic philosophy, and also, in some cases, as that of Cerinthus, of Judaism, with certain elements of Christian doctrine. He also adds: "But I, and whatsoever Christians are orthodox in all things, do know that there will be a resurrection of the flesh, and a thousand years in the city of Jerusalem, built and adorned, and enlarged according to the prophets." He continues: "For thus hath Isaiah spoken of the thousand years: 'for there will be a new heavens and earth.' He then quotes Isaiah 65, making the 'tree of verse 22 the tree of life (or, as we suppose he meant, the restoration of patriarchal longevity to the human race); and adds, 'We believe a thousand years to be figuratively expressed. For it was said to Adam, 'In the day that thou eatest thereof, thou shalt surely die,' Genesis 2:17; so that we know that he did not live a thousand years. We believe, also, that this expression, 'The day of the Lord is as a thousand years,' Psalm 90:4, and 2 Peter 3:8, relates to this." And then, quoting from Revelation 20:1–5, in proof, he says: "We may conclude from many places in Scripture, that those are right who say that 6,000 years is the time fixed for the duration of the present frame of the world."

Eusebius admits that Justin Martyr's writings stood

in high esteem among the early Christians. Also Milner, Semisch, a German writer, and Drs. Cave, Burton, Elliott, and Adam Clark, all confess that this writer held the "chiliasm" of the second century, which constituted so decidedly an article of the Christian faith, to be a criterion of orthodoxy. Also, that "he abounds in solid, sound sense, the product of an acute and well-cultivated mind;" that he was "a witness beyond all exception," and that his learning and piety as such has been testified to by nearly all the succeeding fathers." He was crowned with martyrdom at Rome by being beheaded, A.D. 165.

Irenaeus, bishop of Lyons, was born, it is supposed, near Smyrna, and flourished as a writer between A.D. 176–202. Basil depicts him as "one near the apostles." He was pupil to and trained up under the tutelage of Papias and Polycarp, both of whom were disciples of the Revelator John. For learning, steadfastness, and zeal, he was among the most renowned of the early fathers. Milner highly commends him, and calls him a man of excellent judgment. It may seem to the reader not a little singular, that Professor Shedd, when speaking of Papias, should represent his "mind as comparatively uninfluential, and his writings as of little importance," and quote Eusebius as saying that they "contain matters rather too fabulous," while at the same time he admits that "he was the cause why most of the ecclesiastical writers, urging the antiquity of the man, were carried away by a similar opinion, as, for instance, Irenaeus, or any other that adopted his sentiments." Such statements carry with them their own refutation. It is not in the nature of things, that a man like Irenaeus should have been led to adopt the millenarian system at the hand of a shallow-minded fanatic.

The works of Irenæus, still extant, consist of five books on the heresies of the times. These Mosheim calls "a splendid monument of antiquity." We must here again quote from Professor Shedd. "Irenaeus and Tertullian, in their writings against heretics," says he, "present brief synoptical statements of the authorized faith of the Church; but in none of them do we find the millenarian tenet." Now, let us first put this to the test in reference to Irenaeus. He affirms, that certain heretical opinions had arisen, proceeding from ignorance of the arrangements of God, and the mystery of the first resurrection and the kingdom of the just; and it therefore became needful to speak of them. And, having given a lucid and scriptural exposition of the Abrahamic covenant as embracing in its stipulations, first, Abraham's lineal multitudinous seed, and second, the Gentile nations as blessed through them; and for the security of which, Christ as Abraham's seed was the surety and pledge, he says: "For true and unchangeable is God; wherefore also he said, 'Blessed are the meek, for they shall inherit the earth.'" And to show how fully he supported his prophetical exegeses by quotations from the old and New Testaments, we give the following in his own order of the subjects treated: Isaiah 26:19; Ezekiel 37:12–14; 38:25, 26; Jeremiah 23:7, 8; Isaiah 30:25, 26; 58:14; Luke 12:37–40; Revelation 20:1–6; Isaiah 6:11; Daniel 7:27; Jeremiah 31:10–15; Isaiah 31:9; 32:1; 54:11–14; and 65:17–28.

Dr. Burton, in speaking of these doctrines of Irenaeus, says, that he "goes to the fountain head." He relates it as from John, and John from our Lord. And he adds: "Irenaeus, like Justin [Martyr], calls those 'heretics' who expected the saints' glorification immediately after death and before their resurrection. He also made the Roman kingdom to be the fourth beast described by Daniel, seventh chapter. And on the duration of the world, he says: "In as many days as the world was made, in so many thousand years it is perfected; for if the day of the Lord be as it were a thousand years, and in six days those things that are made were finished; it is manifest that the perfecting of these things is in the six thousandth year, when Antichrist, having reigned 1260 years,...then the Lord shall come from heaven in the clouds with the glory of His Father, casting him and them that obey him into a lake of fire; but bringing to the just the time of the kingdom, that is, the rest, or Sabbath, or seventh day sanctified, and fulfilling to Abraham the promise of the inheritance."

The Churches of Vienna and Lyons addressed an epistle to the Churches in Asia and Phrygia in A.D. 177, which Eusebius inserts at length in his Ecclesiastical History. Professor Moses Stuart thinks it probable that it was written by Irenaeus, though Dr. Elliott ascribes it to one of the Lyonese Christians. After narrating the martyrdoms of Ponticus, a youth of fifteen years, and Blandina, a Christian lady, it says: "The bodies of the martyrs having been contumeliously [contemptuously] treated and exposed for six days, were burned and reduced to ashes, and scattered by the wicked into the Rhone, that not the least particle of them might appear on the earth any more. And they did these things as if they could prevail against God, and prevent their resurrection, and that they might deter others, as they said, 'from the hope of a future life, relying on which, they introduce a strange and new religion, and despise the most extraordinary tortures, and die with joy. Now let us see if they will rise again, and if their God can help them and deliver them out of our hands." Mr. Faber, on this testimony from their enemies of the practical bearing of the doctrine of the resurrection of the body, as held by the primitive martyrs, says: "The doctrine of the literal resurrection of the martyrs prior to that epoch certainly prevailed to a considerable extent throughout the early Church, and often animated the primitive believers to seal the truth with their blood." And on the same subject, the learned Dodwell [Henry Dodwell] writes: "The primitive Christians believed that 'the first resurrection of their bodies would take place in the kingdom of the millennium; and as they considered that resurrection to be peculiar to the just, so they conceived the martyrs would enjoy the principal share of its glory." Irenaeus sealed his testimony with his blood, by being beheaded, under the reign of Severus, in A.D. 202.

Melito, bishop of Sardis, was born in Asia, and was contemporary with Justin Martyr. Tertullian and Polycrates [of Ephesus] both testify to his preeminent piety and eloquence. Besides an *Apology and Canon of the Old Testament*, he wrote a treatise on the Apocalypse. Jerome and Gennadius both affirm that he was a decided millenarian. The time and manner of his death are unknown.

Tertullian was born at Carthage, in Africa, and flourished as a writer between A.D. 196–218. Cyprian thought much of him, and never passed a day without reading some portions of his works. Spanheim calls him "one of the first of the fathers." Others, as Professor Stuart, Mosheim, Neander, and Milner, differ in their estimates of his excellencies and defects. In reference to his views of the Apocalypse, he writes: "We confess that a kingdom is promised us on earth before that in heaven, but in another state, namely, after the resurrection; for it will be one thousand years in a city of divine workmanship, i.e., Jerusalem brought down from heaven; and this city Ezekiel knew, and the apostle John saw. This is the city provided of God to receive the saints in the first resurrection, wherein to refresh them" [not in the "materializing," "gross," and "sensual" pleasures of the elysium of a Cerinthus], but "with an abundance of all spiritual good things, in recompense for those which in the world we have either despised or lost. For it is both just and worthy of God, that his servants should there triumph and rejoice, where they have been afflicted for His name's sake. This is the manner of the heavenly kingdom." Where or how he died is uncertain.

Concerning Clement, bishop of Alexandria, Professor Shedd had come a little nearer the mark, had he claimed Clement of Alexandria as having taken no notice of "the millenarian tenet." Dr. Burnet says: "He has not said anything that I know of, either for or against the millennium: but," he adds, "he takes notice that the seventh day has been accounted sacred both by the Hebrews and Greeks, because of the revolution of the world, and the renovation of all things." And from this Burnet argues, that "it can be in no other sense than that the seventh day represents the seventh millennium, in which the kingdom and renovation are to be." And in his address to the heathen, Clement says: "Therefore Jesus cries aloud, personally urging us, because the kingdom of heaven is at hand: He converts men by fear." "This," says Dr. Duffield, "is Peter's argument (Peter 4:7), and it proves that he regarded the kingdom of heaven, as the prophets testify, to be introduced by judgment: his ideas of that kingdom must have been radically different from those of the spiritualists." And some others regard him as a millenarian. But, be that as it may, although Eusebius calls him an "incomparable master of the Christian philosophy," and Neander attributes to him "great knowledge about divine matters," we regard the preceding as of too equivocal a character to justify the inferences drawn from them. As we have already intimated, Clement, first at the head of the catechetical school (A.D. 188), and then bishop of Alexandria, laid the foundation for that new theory of Scriptural hermeneutics by which the literal interpretation of the prophets was finally "hissed off the stage." We have the explicit declaration of Dr. Murdock, that "he construed the Bible allegorically and fancifully." This with us is decisive. Clement flourished as a writer between A.D. 193–218. Of the place and manner of his death we know nothing.

Methodius, bishop of Olympus, flourished between A.D. 260–312. Dr. Whitby, who was at antipodes [opposite sides] with his sentiments, allows that "Methodius held to a pure millennium, free from everything sensual." He was also admitted by Neander to have been a chiliast. He was a firm opponent of Origen, and charged that fanciful interpreter with heresy. The following passage is quoted from his work by Produs in Epiphaneus: "It is to be expected that at the conflagration, the creation shall suffer a vehement commotion, as if it were about to die: whereby it shall be renovated, and not perish; to the end that we, then also renovated, may dwell in the renewed world free from sorrow. Thus it is said in Psalm 104: 'Thou wilt send forth Thy Spirit, and they shall be created, and Thou wilt renew the face of the earth.' For seeing that after this world there shall be an earth, of necessity there must be inhabitants; and these shall die no more, but be as angels, irreversibly in an incorruptible state, doing all most excellent things." He was crowned with martyrdom, under the emperor Decius, in A.D. 312.

Nepos was a learned Egyptian bishop, and all writers, ancient and modern, admit that he was a millenarian, in which Coracion coincided with him. Dr. Cave says, that "he was a man skilled in the Holy Scriptures, and also a poet; and that he had fallen into the error of the millenarians, and had published books to show that the promises made in the Scriptures to good men, were, according to the sense and opinions of the Jews, to be literally understood." Even Whitby allows that he taught that, "after this (first) resurrection, the kingdom of Christ was to be upon earth for a thousand years, and the saints were to reign with Him. According to Mr. Brooks, "he wrote a book entitled *The Reprehensions of Allegorizers*, which was specially directed against those who now began (A.D. 262) to explain the millennium figuratively."

COMMENCEMENT OF APOSTASY FROM ANCIENT CHILIASM

Having traced the origin of millenarianism through the inspired pre-Christian Hebrew Church, as founded upon the Abrahamic covenant—which was itself but a revised and enlarged form of the first promise of redemption made to fallen man—also that it was recognized by the uninspired Jewish writers, and in the traditional theology of Pagan nations prior to the first coming of Christ; and that it abounds in the epistolary writings of the New Testament age, and constituted the received faith of the Church during the early post-apostolic age: we now approach that period of the commenced apostasy from the said "faith delivered to the saints," as set forth in the following noted prophecy of Paul, 2 Timothy 4:3, 4: "For the time will come when they will not endure sound doctrine; but after their own lusts shall they heap to themselves teachers, having itching ears; and they shall turn their ears from the truth, and shall be turned unto fables."

We have already shown that the millenarian controversy that sprung up in the early part of the third century, was instigated by the introduction into the Church of the new allegorical theory of Origen, in opposition to the literal, as the standard rule of scriptural exegesis.

We have also proved the error of the historical statements alleged by Professor Shedd, to wit: that millenarianism "was not the received faith of the Church certainly down to the year 150;" that "it was held only by individuals;" "that its blooming period was a brief one of about a hundred years;" and "that the third century witnessed a very decided opposition to it." Indeed, the main reliance of anti-millenarians in their assaults upon this system, consists in holding it up to view as a "materializing," "gross," "sensual," and "fanatical heresy," and decrying its followers as a small and insignificant sect. Thus the learned Dr. Hamilton, in his work against the millenarians, says "that its principles were opposed and rejected by almost every father of the Church, with the exception of Barnabas, Clement, Papias, Justin Martyr, Irenaeus, Nepos, Apollinarus, Lactantantius, and Tertullian!" That is, with the exception of all the fathers whom he knows before, and some who were contemporary with and subsequent to, the time of Origen! And this, reader, on the ground that he prefers the fathers of later date, because "their learning and talents far surpassed any in the first centuries of the Church." But we have only to ask, first, what must have been the extent to which millenarianism must have prevailed between the time of John in A.D. 96 and that of Origen in A.D. 232 (the date at which his new allegorical theory first began to obtain in the Church), when all the fathers were its avowed advocates? And second, when, in A.D. 325, at the Council of Nice, 318 bishops, collected from all parts of the Church, incorporated in the Nicene Creed adopted by them, the distinguishing tenets of millenarianism? And finally, third, when Jerome admits that "many Christians and martyrs had affirmed the things which he denied;" and that, toward the close of the fourth century, "a great multitude of Christians agreed with them in his own day?"

But we have also admitted that, after this date, millenarianism began to decline. We have already explained the causes which led to this result. It now comes in place to observe, that this system was not opposed by all on the same grounds. Some writers, as Dionysius, of Alexandria, and Eusebius, of Caesarea, acting on the principle that, if the Apocalypse of John is to be received as canonical, millenarianism is a scriptural doctrine, repudiated that book as spurious. Others, however, of whom Origen was one, while they admitted that it was canonical, and actually declared their belief that the second personal coming of the Lord was imminent in their day, and also admitted that the earth, in its renovated state after the conflagration, would be the seat of the redeemed, yet opposed millenarianism.

Now, how is this to be explained? Simply, we reply, on the ground of their adoption of the Septuagint chronology of the world, in the place of the original Hebrew text. The Septuagint, as we have seen, places the nativity in excess of the Hebrew date at A.M. (Anno Mundi) 5871, which leaves only a fraction over 1,100 years to the close of the 7,000th year from the creation and fall of man. And, as all writers admit that at the close of the seventh chiliad time ends, and the redeemed Church enters upon her eternal state, so the class of interpreters here referred to regulate the commencement of the millennium in accommodation to their variant computations of the Septuagint chronology. Of the chronological calculus of the writers of the early Church, as founded on the Septuagint version, Clement of Alexandria terminated the 6,000 about A.D. 374; Cyprian earlier, in A.D. 243; Eustathius, Lactantius, Hilarion, Jerome, etc., in A.D. 500; Sulpitius Severus, in A.D. 581; and Augustine, in A.D. 650. Indeed, while some of these writers deny any millennium at all, the above system of chronology of those who were anti-millenarian has originated all those theories of a spiritual millennium which have infested the Church from the time of Origen. These theories, one and all, as a matter of course, ignore that fundamental principle of millenarianism, i.e., the literal restoration, conversion, and national preeminence of the Jews, and the blessing of the Gentile nations through them, together with the personal reign of Christ and His saints over the saved nations in the flesh for a thousand years. And yet, singular as it may appear, while all the spiritualizing theorists rightly place the universal conflagration of the earth at the end of the seventh chiliad, some otherwise able expositors of millenarianism, by confounding the judgments of God upon the wicked at the commencement of the millennial era with that event, erroneously represent it as pre-millennial. Several of the ancient fathers, together with those of modern date, have fallen into this mistake. On the other hand, anti-millenarians, both ancient and modern, in one form or another, have incorporated in their theories one or other of the distinguishing tenets of millenarianism. Thus Jerome. "God will make new heavens and a new earth: not other heavens and another earth; but the former ones changed into better." And even as late as Gregory the Great, we find him saying: "Others are not to be created, but the same renewed." And again, on Ecclesiastes 3:14, he says: "They will pass as to their present figure or appearance, but as to their substance, they will remain forever." And so Origen. In the thirteenth book of his work against Celsus, he says: "We do not deny the purging fire of the destruction of wickedness, and the renovation of all things." And again: "The earth, after its conflagration, shall become habitable again and be the mansion of men." And finally, he affirms in his thirteenth Homily on Jeremiah, "If any man shall preserve the washing of the Holy Spirit, he shall have his part in the first resurrection: Let us lay the Scriptures to heart, that we may be raised up with the saints, and have our lot with Jesus Christ."

But the question is, did the above facts make these writers millenarians? Our reply is, by no means. Though they are cardinal points in that system, yet, this amalgamating of the allegorical with the literal in the interpretation of "the teachings of Isaiah and John respecting the second coming of Christ," strikes at the very vitals of that system. For, the order of events, as well as the nature of the things predicted, being founded on the chronology of the Septuagint, aims to "sweep from off the stage" the last vestiges of the "chiliasm" of the Church.

We are not ambitious, therefore, to augment the number of millenarians by accessions from the ranks of such. The preceding remarks are predicated of the conviction that the time has fully come, when there is a need to distinguish between things which differ in these premises. Our object and aim is to present millenarianism before the Churches of this day on its merits as a whole according to "the law and the testimony" of Holy Writ. On this subject, we are willing to hold to the issue in accordance with what Origen himself admits: that "they who deny millenarianism, are they who interpret the sayings of the prophets by a figure of speech; but they who assert it are styled disciples of the letter of Scripture only." With these explanations, which the reader will do well to keep in view, we now resume the thread of our history.

Notwithstanding Professor Shedd's confident statement, that "Dionysius, bishop of Alexandria, succeeded by force of argument in repressing a very gross form of millenarianism that was spreading in his diocese;" yet, that the chiliastic party was still strong after this, is evident from the declaration of Burnet, that "we do not find that Dionysius's opposition had any great effect." He also states that "the millennial kingdom of Christ was the general doctrine of the primitive Church from the times of the apostles to the Council of Nice, inclusively."

Epiphanius, bishop of Constantia or Salamis in

Cyprus, and who flourished between A.D. 367–403, was a millenarian, and testifies that the doctrine was held by many in his time. Quoting the words of Paulinus, bishop of Antioch, concerning one Vitalius, whom he highly commends for his piety, orthodoxy, and learning, he says, "Moreover, others have affirmed that the venerable man would say, that in the first resurrection we shall accomplish a certain millenary of years;" on which Epiphanius observes, "And that indeed this millenary term is written in the Apocalypse of John, and is received of very many of them that are godly, is manifest. Besides, in A.D. 402, he vehemently contended against the Originists." But from his time, millenarianism began to grow unpopular, and to fall into general disuse.

Hilary, bishop of Poictiers, A.D. 368, Ambrose, bishop of Milan, A.D. 374–397, Chrysostom, bishop of Constantinople, A.D. 370–407, and Jerome of Rome, A.D. 363–420, all of the Origenist school, form the connecting links between Epiphanius and Augustine, bishop of Hippo, A.D. 390–430. While the Church was now becoming more and more corrupted by the growing superstitions of the age, and the doctrines of grace continued to degenerate, Augustine remained comparatively free from the one and a zealous advocate of the other, and, as Milner says, "the light from his writings glimmered through many ages, down even to the Reformation." He was once a chiliast, but owing to its perversion by many and the misrepresentations of his enemies, he abandoned it, and adopting the Septuagint chronology, developed what is usually called the Augustinian Theory of the millennium, which afterwards became very prevalent, and which formed a new era in its history. The world's duration he accordingly made six-millennial, and affirmed that the resurrection was spiritual, which he dated from the first coming of Christ, and with the other anti-millenarian fathers of the fourth and fifth centuries, explained the seventh sabbatical day, not of a seventh sabbatical millennium of rest, but an eternal sabbath—a view generally adopted afterwards.

But in regard to the millenarian faith of the early Church, Dr. Lardner, though an anti-millenarian, testifies, "The millennium has been a favorite doctrine of some ages, and has had the patronage of the learned as well as the vulgar among Christians." Chillingworth says: "Whatever doctrine is taught by the fathers of any age, not as doctors, but as witnesses of the doctrine of the Church of their time, neither did any contradict them in it; ergo, it is doubtless to be esteemed." Again he says: "It appears manifest out of this book of Irenaeus, that the doctrine of the chiliasts was in his judgment apostolic tradition, as also it was esteemed (for nothing appears to the contrary) by all the doctors, and saints, and martyrs of, or about his time; for all that speak of it, or whose judgments in the point are any way recorded, are for it; and Justin Martyr professeth, that all good and orthodox Christians of his time believed it, and those that did not, he reckons among heretics." Mosheim gives substantially the same testimony. Bishop Russell says: "The Jews and their followers, in primitive times, understood the millennium literally; the word had no double sense in their creed; it was not in their estimation the emblem or shadow of better things to come; on the contrary, it denoted the actual visible appearance of the Messiah, and the establishment of his kingdom upon earth as the Sovereign of the elect people of God." Dr. Burton says: "It cannot be denied that Papias, Irenaeus, Justin Martyr, and all the other ecclesiastical writers, believed, literally that the saints would rise in the first resurrection, and reign with Christ upon earth previous to the general resurrection." Dr. Neander, speaking of the early Church, says: "They were accustomed to consider that...as the world was created in six days, and according to Psalm 90:4, a thousand years in God's sight is but as one day, so the world was supposed to endure 6,000 years in its present condition; and as the Sabbath day was the day of rest, so this millennial reign was to form the seven thousandth year period of the world's existence, at the close of the whole temporal dispensation connected with the world."

Quotations to the same effect might be made from other anti-millenarian writers, but with all those "whose respect for everything Catholic and ecclesiastical," like that of Eusebius, is "very high," and who are wont to retreat to the fountain head of early post-apostolic antiquity in support of their favorite theories, the above testimony of their anti-millenarian peers in regard to the faith of the primitive "chiliasts," is specially commended to their respectful consideration.

MILLENARIANISM DURING THE MEDIEVAL AGE

We now enter upon the long and dreary interval of the dark ages. Yes, "the blooming age of millenarianism was destined to pass away. That "falling away first" (the apostasy) which was to be headed up in the revelation of "the man of sin as the precursor of the second coming of our Lord, and which is called "the mystery of iniquity," began to work in Paul's time. The very phraseology indicates that it was to take place within the Church, which of course implies that, during this dispensation, she was to be of a mixed character, analogous to the wheat and tares in the parable, both of which were to "grow together until the harvest."

And we affirm that this apostasy from "the faith at first delivered to the saints" was to consist, especially, of a perversion and denial of the doctrine of our blessed Lord's second personal coming, as embraced in the tenets of millenarianism. When speaking of His second coming to avenge His elect of their adversaries, as illustrated in the parable of the judge and the importunate widow seeking redress at his hand, Christ said, "Nevertheless, when the Son of Man cometh, shall He find (this) faith on the earth?" So far from it, in spite of her boasted "orthodoxy" in other respects, the apostate portion of the nominal Church, "walking after their own lusts," will be found uttering the demand of Peter's predicted "scoffers of the last days, saying, where is the promise of his coming?"

We hold that the tenets of millenarianism as a matter of divine revelation, are infallible and immutable. Not so with its uninspired advocates, whether ancient or modern. They were both fallible and mutable. In regard therefore to the ancient fathers, while we hold them to be credible witnesses of what was believed in their time, we discard them as authority as to what should be believed. Still we maintain that, in all the fundamental principles of that system, however they may have erred in its details, they interpreted "the teachings of Isaiah and John concerning the second coming of Christ" according to "the mind of the Spirit."

We concede, then, that the "gold, silver, and precious stones" of millenarian truth in these early times, were more or less tarnished by the "wood, hay, and stubble" of man's device. Hence these latter, in the way and manner already indicated, were seized upon and used by all classes and grades of anti-millenarians, as the weapons to "turn away men's ears from the truth, and to turn them unto fables." And when we consider that, along with the gradual decay of millenarianism, the insidious working of a horde of rapacious, ambitious, and aspiring ecclesiastics was inundating the Church with every species of error in doctrine and corruption of the primitive usages of the Church, and especially after the time of Constantine down to that of Augustine, nothing remained in order to mature that apostasy, but the engrafting into the theology of the Church the theory of *that father* respecting the millennium. The old system of Paganism had indeed fallen, but at the opening of the fifth century the Papacy was hastening to its birth, and, by the edict of Justinian I, was ushered into being in the person of John II, the then Patriarch of Rome, A.D. 533, as the so-called vicegerent of Jesus Christ upon earth. Henceforth the ecclesiastical "little horn" of the Papacy (and which soon after became an ecclesiastico-political power) commenced to "make war with the saints, and to prevail against them;" and that, on the ground of their chiliastic protestations against the corrupt Church of Rome as antichristian, and the Pope as Antichrist.

For this consummation, Origen, who made the Church on earth "the mystic kingdom of heaven," and Eusebius, who spoke of it as "the very image of the kingdom of

Christ," and Augustine, who invested it with the appropriate form and proportions of a regular system, had prepared the way. "It is worthy of remark," says Bishop Russell, "that so long as the prophecies regarding the millennium were interpreted literally, the Apocalypse was received as an inspired production, and as the work of the apostle John; but no sooner did theologians find themselves compelled to view its annunciations through the medium of allegory and metaphorical description, than they ventured to call in question its heavenly origin, its genuineness, and its authority. Dionysius, the great supporter of the allegorical school, gives a decided opinion against the authenticity of the Revelation." On the other hand, Eunapius the Pagan, even in A.D. 396, speaking of the martyr-worship in the Church of Rome, exclaimed, "These are the gods that the earth now a days brings forth; these the intercessors with the gods—men called martyrs: before whose bones and skulls, pickled and salted, the monks kneel and lie prostrate, covered with filth and dust." But the augmented corruptions and abominations of the Papal See of Rome during the fifth and sixth centuries, while they made the Pagan to blush, cast into the shade all that had preceded them. Can we then be surprised, that under such circumstances, the true millennium was cast aside, and with it the Apocalypse that taught it? "Rome," says Dr. Burnet, "always had an evil eye on the millennium," i.e., as taught by the chiliasts. Baronius, a Roman Catholic historian of the sixteenth century, in alluding to the chiliasm of the fifth century writes: "The figments of the millenaries being rejected everywhere, and derided by the learned with hisses and laughter, and being also put under the ban, were entirely destroyed!"

But why this opposition of the Church of Rome to chiliasm? Let Dr. Burnet reply. "I never yet met with a Popish doctor that held the millennium...It did not suit the scheme which they had drawn. The Apocalypse of John supposed the true Church under hardships and persecutions; but the Church of Rome supposing Christ reigns already by his Vicar, the Pope, hath been in prosperity and greatness, and the commanding Church in Christendom for a long time. And the millennium being properly a reward and a triumph for those that come out of persecution (i.e., the martyrs); such as have lived always in pomp and prosperity, can pretend to no share in it, or be benefited by it. This has made the Church of Rome always have an evil eye upon this doctrine, because it seemed to have an evil eye upon her; and as she grew in splendor and greatness, she eclipsed and obscured it more and more; so that it would have been lost out of the world, as an obsolete error, if it had not been revived by some at the Reformation." And so, we add, just in proportion as the Protestant Churches of Christendom have been exempted from persecution, and have increased in worldly prosperity, have they, under one form or another, looked with an evil eye upon this doctrine." Protestants, think of this!

But what theory did the Church of Rome substitute in the place of chiliasm? It was that of Augustine, as already explained, and which was adopted and expounded in the apocalyptic writings of Tichonius of the fourth century; Primasius of the sixth; Andreas of the sixth or seventh; Ambrose, Anabert, and probably Bede of the eighth; and Berengard of the ninth. Elliott, in his *Horae Apocalypticae*, gives the following scheme of it: "That the millennium of

Satan's binding, and the saints reigning, dated from Christ's ministry, when he beheld Satan fall like lightning from heaven; it being meant to signify his triumph over Satan in the hearts of true believers; and that the subsequent figuration of Gog and Magog indicated the coming of Antichrist at the end of the world—the 1,000 years being a figurative numeral, expressive of the whole period intervening. It supposed the resurrection taught to be that of dead souls from the death of sin to the life of righteousness; the beast conquered by the saints, meant the wicked world; its image, a hypocritical profession; the resurrection being continuous, till the end of time, when the universal resurrection and final judgment would take place."

But if, as Baronius affirms, "the figments of the millenaries were entirely exterminated" in the fifth century, how is it that it was revived at the Reformation? The fact is, the learned Romanist, like some others, committed a slight error in this matter. He happened to overlook the historic fact, in reference to the ancient Vaudois, or Waldenses (Adherents of a church tradition that began as an ascetic movement within Western Christianity before the Reformation), that heroic band of faithful "witnesses" for the truth, who descended from those ancient sufferers under the Pagan emperors, that sought for refuge from the hand of their bloody persecutors in the remote regions of the Cottian Alps, and who are known to exist down to the present day, in the secluded and extensive valleys at the foot of the Alps in the northwest corner of Piedmont.

Now, these ancient Vaudois form the connecting link between the New Testament and early post-Christian Church; and the primitive doctrines to which they adhered were preserved uncorrupt, through the Albigenses, the Lollards or Wicklifites, the Bohemian Protestants, etc., who derived those doctrines from them, down to the time of the Reformation. If any doubt this, we would refer them to the following testimony from Romish writers themselves. Thus: Pope Alexander III, when presiding over the Synod of Tours in A.D. 1167, pronounced the doctrine of the Vaudois to be "a damnable heresy of long standing." Another synod held at La Vaux, urged the Pope to exterminate "an heretical pest" (meaning the Vaudois), "generated in olden times, of enormous growth and great antiquity." The Romish inquisitor, Reinerus Sacco, having expressed alarm at the danger which threatened his church from the heresy of the Vaudois, declared that it was "because it was more ancient than any other, as well as more general." And Cassini, a Franciscan, writing in the sixteenth century against the Vaudois, says, "The errors of the Vaudois consist in their denial that the Romish is the Holy Mother Church, and in their refusal to obey her traditions." And he then adds, "In other points, they recognize the Church of Christ; and for my part," says he, "I cannot deny that they have always been members of the Church."

Now, one of the principal articles of faith of these Vaudois is, that "they have always regarded the Papal Church as Antichrist: the Babylon of the Apocalypse;" and "they also condemned the mystical or allegorical interpretations of Scripture." Of course, then, they must have interpreted literally "the teachings of Isaiah and John concerning the second coming of Christ," the millennium, etc. Their writings consist of a *Treatise on Antichrist*, and the *Noble Lesson*, the last written in the twelfth century, and both pronounced by the best judges to be genuine and authentic. We have not space for further extracts. Suffice it to say, that they are purely millenarian.

We would add on this subject, that the Rev. Mr. Gilly, a distinguished Episcopal clergyman, in his valuable and instructive account of the Vaudois or Waldenses, whom he visited in A.D. 1823, gives a report of a conversation that he then had with M. Peyrani, the Moderator of their Church. This minister of Christ having felt great satisfaction in explaining how closely the doctrines of the Vaudois Church assimilate to those of the Church of England (i.e., the Thirty-nine Articles),...with conscious and becoming pride he said, "But remember, that you are indebted to us for your emancipation from Papal bondage. We led the way. We stood in the first rank, and against us the first thunderbolts of Rome were fulminated. The bayings of the bloodhounds of the inquisition were heard in our valleys before you knew its name. They hunted down some of our ancestors, and pursued others from glen to glen, and over rock and mountain, till they obliged us to take shelter in foreign countries. A few of these wanderers penetrated as far as Provence and Languedoc, and from them were derived the Albigenses, or (so called) heretics of Albi. The province of Guienne afforded shelter to the Albigenses. Guienne was then in your possession. From an English province, our doctrines found their way into England itself, and your Wicklif preached nothing more than what had been advanced by the ministers of our valleys 400 years before his time."

With this account of the preparation of the way for the commencement of the great Continental and Anglican

Reformation, we proceed.

REVIVAL OF MODERN MILLENARIANISM

In this portion of his *History of Christian Doctrine*, Professor Shedd affects to dispose of "millenarianism or chiliasm" in a very summary manner. He says, "The history of chiliasm since the Reformation, presents few points of importance. During the present century, individual minds in England and America, and upon the continent of Europe, have attempted to revive the theory—in some instances, in union with an intelligent and earnest orthodoxy; in others, in connection with an uneducated and somewhat fanatical pietism. The first class is represented by Delitzsch and Auberlin in Germany, and by Cumming, Elliott, and Bonar in Great Britain; the second class by the so called Adventists and Millerites in the United States." For the sake of convenience, we shall divide the period above indicated into three parts:

The first period is from the Reformation, which commenced in A.D. 1517, down to A.D. 1550, embracing an interval of 33 years. One remark on the above passage, however, before passing on. Professor Shedd makes a distinction between those chiliasts who have flourished since the Reformation, some possessing "an intelligent and earnest orthodoxy," while others were "uneducated and somewhat fanatical." But to what, we ask, does this distinction amount, if the "chiliasm" itself of a "Delitzsch," an "Auberlin," a "Cumming," an "Elliott" and a "Bonar," is identical with "the so-called Adventists and Millerites"? In other words, if chiliasm or millenarianism was "the invention of Cerinthus" of the first century—in proof of which Professor Shedd quotes the declaration of Gaius (Caius?) of the second century—then what does it matter whether its advocates were of the "first" or "the second class"? In either case, the system is equally "materializing," "gross," "sensual," "fanatical," and "heretical"! What will the millenarians of the day at home and abroad think of this estimate of their "intelligence and earnest orthodoxy" by Professor Shedd? But no. While we have demonstrated, from the origin of millenarianism, and its distinctive tenets in all ages, the fallacy of its alleged identity with the unscriptural, sensual, and delusive theory of the arch-heretic Cerinthus, and of the fanaticism of the Anabaptists, fifth-monarchy men, and others since his time, on the one hand; we have shown that the "intelligence and earnest orthodoxy" of those who willfully and resolutely reject it, cannot save them from the imputation of heresy, on the other.

But, "the history of chiliasm since the Reformation, presents few points of importance." Indeed! We, however, Doctor, are not quite so sure of that. In regard, then, to the Reformation, we concede that it was a great and glorious achievement, under God, in arousing Christendom to a sight and sense of the enormities of that masterpiece of satanic device for the destruction of the bodies and souls of men, the ecclesiastico-political despotism of Papal Rome. But, on two points, the following facts will prove that the Church of the present day is in capital error in reference to that work. The first relates to its extent, and the results growing out of it. It is to be recollected, that the Reformation, Continental and Anglican combined, contrary to the general opinion regarding it, extended to only about one third part of

Christendom. And as to its final results, reaching down to this day, the historian Macaulay, a prince among Protestants, affirms that, "during the past 250 years, Protestantism has made no conquests worth speaking of. Nay, we believe," he adds, "that as far as there has been a change, that change has been in favor of the Church of Rome." This fact stands connected with and furnishes proof of the other error, to wit, that the Church of this day—which maintains that the world is to be converted during this age, to be followed by a millennium of pious rulers in the flesh, under the spiritual reign of Christ—occupies the same platform with that of the reformers. So far from it, the great Luther himself, in his comment on the passage, "Other sheep I have," says: "Some, in explaining this passage, say, that before the latter days, the whole world shall become Christian. This is a falsehood, forged by Satan, that he might darken sound doctrine, that we might not rightly understand it. Beware, therefore, of this delusion."

It is true, nevertheless, that, during the sixteenth century, considerable attention was devoted to the exposition of the prophecies. First and foremost in the ranks was the renowned Luther. His views of the Apocalypse, however, were somewhat meager and obscure. On the millennium, Dr. Elliott observes, he endorsed the Augustinian system, somewhat modified, and made it the 1,000 years between John and the issuing forth of the Turks; and in the language of Bengel, "he believed also, with many others, that the duration of the world, from its commencement, would be only 6,000 years; and hence considered its end so near, that he could see no space for any future millennium." Other writers adopted substantially the views of Luther, e.g., Melancthon, who flourished A.D. 1514–1560; Piscator, Professor of Theology at Strasbourg, 1530–1546; Osiander, one of Luther's first disciples, 1530–1552; Flacius, Professor of the Greek and Latin Languages at Wittenberg, and a pupil of Luther and Melancthon, 1561–1575; Chytraeus, of Rostock, who wrote a commentary on the Apocalypse, 1590–1600; Bullinger, of Zurich, 1531–1575; and Pareus, of Silesia, who also wrote an Apocalyptic commentary, 1590–1622. Then, too, there was the celebrated reformer, John Calvin, of Geneva, in Switzerland, who flourished between A.D. 1532–1564. He repudiates the millennium, rebuking those (the chiliasts) who would limit the kingdom to a thousand years; but with Luther—in opposition to the post-millennialists of the present day—he looked for a renewed earth, saying, "I expect, with St. Paul, a reparation of all the evils caused by sin, for which he represents the creatures as groaning and travailing;" and also allows that "the Scriptures most commonly exhibit the resurrection of the children of God alone, in connection with the glory of heaven, because, strictly speaking, Christ will come, not for the destruction of the world, but for purposes of salvation."

According to this theory, therefore, these writers maintain that at the commencement of the seventh chiliad, Christ was to personally appear as Judge, raise the dead, reward His saints, punish the wicked, and introduce His Church into her eternal state. They have overlooked the circumstance, so emphatically stated by John, of "the first resurrection" of the righteous dead, as separated from "the rest of the dead which lived not again till the thousand years (or seventh chiliad) were finished" (Revelation 20:1–6); and also the equal delivering up of the kingdom (millennial) to God the Father, as stated by Paul, 1 Corinthians 15:14–28.

They were, consequently, one and all, anti-millenarians. Their minds, being trammeled with the Augustinian theory, it was reserved in the providence of God as the work more especially of the Anglican Reformers, to revive and recover to the Church that long-lost truth. Passing on, therefore, we come to take a bird's-eye glance at the prophetical expositions of the English Reformers. First and foremost among them was Cranmer, archbishop of Canterbury, who flourished between A.D. 1533–1556. With him were associated Latimer and Ridley.

Hugh Latimer was raised to the bishopric of Worcester by Henry VIII, in A.D. 1535, but soon after resigned. In his third sermon on the Lord's Prayer, he speaks of "a parliament in which Christ shall bear rule, and not man; and which the righteous pray for when they say, 'Thy kingdom come,' because they know that therein reformation of all things shall be had;'" and he adds, "Let us therefore have a desire that this day may come quickly." It is also here to be specially noted that Latimer, with the other English reformers, were among the first to abandon the Septuagint for that of the Shorter Hebrew Chronology. Hence, in the same sermon, he continues: "The world was ordained to endure (as all learned men affirm, and prove from Scripture) 6,000 years. Now of that number there be past 5,552 years; so that there is no more left but 448 years. And further more," he adds, "those days shall be shortened: it shall not be full 6,000 years; 'the days shall be shortened for the elect's sake.'"...Then, he continues, "There will be great alterations in day; there will be hurly-burly [confusion], like as we see when a man dieth. There will be such alterations of the earth and elements, they will lose their former nature, and be endued with another nature. And then shall they see the Son of Man come in a cloud, with power and great glory. Certain it is that He shall come to judge; but we cannot tell the [exact] time when He shall come." And again: In his sermon for the second Sunday in Advent, after saying that the saints in that day "shall be taken up to meet Christ in the air, and so shall come down with Him again," he adds, "That man or that woman that saith these words, 'Thy kingdom come,' with a faithful heart, no doubt desireth in very deed that God will come to judgment, and amend all things in this world, and put down Satan, that old serpent, under our feet."

Now, what is this, we ask, but pure millenarianism! First: Speaking of the change that will take place in "the earth and elements," he says that "great alterations" will be made "in that day;" meaning, doubtless, not such as will be effected by the last conflagration, but the restoration of "the earth and elements" to that paradisiacal state indicated in the prophecy of Isaiah, chapter 65:17, 18, and 66:20–24. Second: As to his chronology, by adding 5,552 + 448 = 6,000 years, which, according to his computation, would end in A.D. 1983. But, the "shortening of the days," of which he speaks, is, we submit, misplaced. He overlooked, as have all chronologists until within the last half century or so, the discrepancy in the historic chronology of the Old Testament for the period between the exodus and the fourth year of Solomon, as given in 1 Kings 6:1, and Acts 13:17–22, and which, when properly adjusted, adds 128 years to the 480 years of 1 Kings 6:1. This, when supplemented to the A.M. 4004, which is the date of Archbishop Usher for the nativity, carries forward the true date of that event to A.M. 4132, and places the terminus of the 6000 years at A.D. 1868. And finally, third: Latimer rightly makes the rapture of the risen and changed living saints at the second coming of the Lord, to take place at the same time with the binding of Satan at the commencement of "the thousand years."

Nicholas Ridley, bishop of London, was a companion of Latimer. In his *Lamentation for the Change of Religion*, written in A.D. 1554, he says: "The world, without doubt—this I do believe, and therefore I say it—draws toward an end. Let us, with John, the servant of God, cry in our hearts unto our Savior Christ, 'Come, Lord Jesus, come!'" He here comprehends in a few words all that is set forth in the above extracts from Latimer. He, with his companion Latimer, suffered martyrdom at the stake, under the bloody reign of Queen Mary, in A.D. 1555.

We come now to note a very extraordinary coincidence in the history of "chiliasm," between the early part of the fourth century, and that which marked the state of things connected with it in the middle of the sixteenth century. In regard to the first, Professor Shedd tells us that "Lactantius (330) is the only man of any note in the fourth century who defends the system." Whereas we have shown, that at the Council of Nice, held in A.D. 325, and which was composed of some 318 bishops, collected from all parts of Christendom, the "Nicene Creed" then drawn up by them, concludes with that extract from it which we have inserted with an English translation and which contains a declaration of the purest chiliastic tenets. So now again in the middle of the sixteenth century, although the learned Professor positively affirms that "the history of chiliasm since the Reformation presents few points of importance," yet we find that, in exact harmony with the millenarianism of Latimer and Ridley, the same doctrine is most lucidly and fully set forth in the Catechism of Edward VI, in the last year of his reign (May 20, 1553), of which catechism, endorsed by the king himself, Bishop Burnet declares that Cranmer owned that he was the author.

Edmund Sandys was archbishop of York in Queen Elizabeth's time. He flourished between A.D. 1550–1588. In his sermon on "The end of all things is at hand," says: "As His (Christ's) coming is most certain, so the hour, day, month, and year is most uncertain. Now, as we know not the day and the time, so let us be assured this coming of the Lord is near...That it is at hand, may be probably gathered out of the Scriptures. The signs mentioned by Christ in the gospel" [see Luke 21:24–31], "which should be the foreshadows of this terrible day, are almost already all fulfilled."

The next in order is the Westminster Assembly of Divines, convened by Parliament during the reign of Charles I, in A.D. 1543. They were appointed to frame *The Directory for Public Worship*, *The Confession of Faith*, *The Larger and Shorter Catechisms*, and to sign *The Solemn League and Covenant*. Besides 10 lords and 20 commoners, there were 121 divines, Episcopalians, Presbyterians, and Independents. Now, while it is not pretended that this learned "assembly" did incorporate into the *Confession of Faith* or the *Catechisms* compiled by them the tenets of millenarianism, yet Brooks, Anderson, Duffield and others affirm that a majority of the "chief divines" of that body were millenarians. Indeed, Robert Bailee, one of the members, and a strong anti-millenarian, writing to his friend William Spang at that time, admits that "the most of the chief divines here, not only Independents, but others, such as Twiss (who was moderator of the assembly), Marshall, Palmer, and many more, are express chiliasts." Among these "many more," were such men as the celebrated John Selden, the erudite Henry Ainsworth, D.D., the learned Thomas Gataker, the admired Daniel Featly, D.D., Thomas Goodwin, Jeremiah Burroughs, Joseph Caryll, Simeon Ash, William Bridge, A.M., William Gouge, D.D., J. Langley, and Peter Sterry. To these we may add Rev. William Perkins, rector of St. Andrew's parish, England, who flourished between A.D. 1580 and 1602.

On the other hand, Fox, the martyrologist, and who also wrote a commentary on the Revelation, was the first modern writer who made the binding of Satan for a thousand years to commence from the time of Constantine. He was born in A.D. 1517, and died in A.D. 1587. And Thomas Brightman, rector of Hawns, England, between A.D. 1585–1600, who also wrote an exposition of the Apocalypse, followed in the track of Fox.

And finally, in reference to this period, we shall claim that dauntless reformer and founder of the Presbyterian Church in Scotland, John Knox, whose prayers, Queen Mary said, she feared more than an army of 20,000 men, as a chiliast. On the doctrine of the earth's renovation, Knox writes: "To reform the face of the whole earth, which never was, nor yet shall be till the righteous King and Judge appear for the restoration of all things." Acts 3:21. In his letter to the faithful in London, dated 1554, he, on the Redeemer's advent, asks: "Has not the Lord Jesus, in despite of Satan's malice, carried up our flesh into heaven and shall He not return? We know He shall return, and that with expedition."

What now says the reader of the above interval from the time of Luther in A.D. 1517? Is he prepared to endorse Professor Shedd's statement, that "the history of chiliasm since the Reformation presents few points of importance?" But we proceed to consider, briefly, the next period: from the middle of the sixteenth to the eighteenth century, embracing an interval of 150 years. In his history, the Professor says: "During the present century, individual minds in England and America, and upon the continent of Europe, have attempted to revive the theory." Besides, then, that the Professor totally ignores the historic facts connected with the preceding revival of chiliasm from Luther's time, he also would limit said revival to attempts made by a few "individual minds," e.g., "Delitzsch and Auberlin in Germany, and Cumming, Elliott, and Bonar, in Great Britain," etc., "during the present century!" If, however, the learned Professor had penetrated the pages of history about fifty years farther back, he might have hit upon such a millenarian as the profoundly learned Joseph Mede, B.D., styled "the illustrious Mede," who flourished as a writer between A.D. 1612 and 1638. His principal work is the *Clavis Apocalyptical*, of which, in connection with his other works, Dr. Elliott says, that they "have generally been thought to constitute an era in the solution of the Apocalyptic mysteries," and "for which," particularly his *Clavis Apocalypticae*, "he has been looked upon and written of as a man almost inspired."

The biographer of Mede assures us, "that he tried all ways imaginable to place the millennium elsewhere than after the first resurrection, and, if it were possible, to begin it at the reign of Constantine. But after all his striving, he was forced to yield." And he says of himself: "When I first perceived that millennium to be a state of the Church consequent of the times of the beast, I was averse from a proper acceptation of that resurrection (i.e., of Revelation 20:4, 5), taking it for a rising of the Church from a dead estate" (which has formed the basis of interpretation of all orders of anti-millenarian allegorists from the time of Origen to the present day); "yet afterward," he says, "more seriously considering and weighing all things, I found no ground or footing for any sense but the literal." Our space will not allow for even a synopsis of his scheme. It must suffice to remark, that while his system of interpretation was founded upon the "all scripture given by inspiration of God," or that "testimony of Jesus which is the spirit of prophecy;" his writings furnish the most ample evidence of his extensive, if not indeed unexampled familiarity with the fathers of antiquity, both Christian and Jewish. And, although we do not set up the claim of inspiration on his behalf as an interpreter of "the teachings of Isaiah and John concerning the second coming of Christ;" yet, from his acquaintance with all the extant theories, both true and false, from the earliest times down to his day, he may be said to approach nearer to "the mind of the Spirit" than that of any other. It has hence been truly said of him, that his works have done more to revive the study of the prophecies, and to furnish guides to others in promoting millenarianism, than any other one man before or since his day.

We leave the reader therefore to decide as to the consistency or justness of Dr. Shedd in this attempt to cast such a chiliastic writer into the shade. Why, Delitzsch and Auberlin, in Germany, and Cumming, Elliott, and Bonar, in England, were and are but the copyists, so to speak, of Joseph Mede. Nor they only. Other millenarians sat at his feet as did Paul at the feet of Gamaliel. Dr. William Twiss, A.D. 1625, in a letter to him, writes: "Mr. Mede, I would willingly spend my days in hanging upon your lips," etc., "to hear you discourse upon the glorious kingdom of Christ here on earth, to begin with the ruin of antichrist." So too the erudite Archbishop Usher, though somewhat shy of committing himself on the subject, yet observes of Mede's work on the Apocalypse, "I cannot sufficiently commend it." The fact is, that Usher, though for a time trammeled with the Augustinian theory, yet Mr. Mede, in writing to Dr. Twiss, says of him, that "he did not discover any aversion or opposition to the notion I represented to him thereabout." And Mr. Wood told Mr. Mede, after the archbishop had read his (Mede's) papers, that he said, "I hope we shall meet together in *resurrectio prima.*"

So also the Rev. Robert Maton, minister and commoner at Oxford, A.D. 1642; the Rev. Thomas Adams, a learned tutor in Cromwell's time, A.D. 1650; the seraphic poet, Milton, A.D. 1660; the Rev. James Janeway, a dissenting divine of Oxford, A.D. 1660; and Bishop Jeremy Taylor, though he condemned the early chiliastic belief, yet most inconsistently; for, while he admits the catholicity of the doctrine, he maintains in his writings a cardinal point in pre-millenarianism, as may be seen from the following: "The resurrection," he says, "shall be universal; good and bad shall rise; yet not all together: but first Christ then we that are Christ's—and then there is another resurrection... they that are not his: 'Blessed and holy is he that hath a part in the first resurrection.' There is a first and a second resurrection, even after this life." So also the Rev. Thomas Watson, in A.D. 1670, and the famous Richard Baxter, minister of Kidderminster, in A.D. 1670–1691. Besides other passages in his writings, which indicate the leaning of his mind favorably to the chiliastic tenets, but yet undecided "about the thousand years' reign of Christ on earth before the final judgment;" "yet I must say," he adds, "that I cannot confute what such learned men as Mr. Mede, Dr. Twiss, and others (after the old fathers) have hereof asserted...But I believe there will be new heavens and earth, on which will dwell righteousness.

If our space would allow, to the above scores of other witnesses might be added, who bore the most emphatic testimony to the pre-millennial doctrine during the seventeenth century. True, in A.D. 1657, Dr. Holmes's chiliastic work, published in 1654, under the title of *The Resurrection Revealed*," was virulently attacked by Thomas Hall, B. D., pastor of Kingsnorton, England. But we have the testimony of Dr. Adam Clarke, in reference to a work on the Revelation by that Scottish nobleman Lord John Napier, issued about A.D. 1575 or 1580, and in which he advocated the near coming of the Lord, that, "so very plausible were the reasonings and calculations of Lord Napier, that there was scarcely a Protestant in Europe who read his works (i.e., at the opening of this century), who was not of the same opinion."

Accordingly, the writings of the most eminent divines

of this century not avowedly chiliastic, were so tinged with its tenets, as to render them utterly irreconcilable either with the anti-millenarian or post-millennial theories. Such was the case with Isaac Ambrose, a divine of some notoriety in England in A.D. 1650. And, though Samuel Rutherford, professor of divinity at St. Andrew's in Scotland, who flourished between A.D. 1643 and 1661, is claimed by both parties, yet the following never can be reconciled with the present popular views of the conversion of the world before the second coming of Christ. He says: "The Lord's Bride will be up and down, above the water swimming, and under the water sinking, until her lovely and mighty Redeemer and Husband set His head through those skies, and come with His fair court to settle all their disputes and give them the hoped-for inheritance." Again he says, on the doctrine of Christ's personal reign, that the Church ought to "avouch the royal crown and absolute supremacy of our Lord Jesus Christ, 'the Prince of the kings of the earth,' as becometh; for certain it is Christ will reign the Father's King in Mount Zion, and his sworn covenant will not be buried." And, on the bringing in of Israel, he says: "Oh for a sight in this flesh of mine of the prophesied marriage between Christ and them." And of the in-gathering of the Gentiles, he adds, "The kings of Tarshish, and of the isles, must bring presents to our Lord Jesus," etc..."It is our part to pray, that the kingdoms of the earth may become Christ's." Now, these sentiments are purely millenarian.

The same holds true of the general character of other writers, e.g., Thomas Vincent, a dissenting minister of London between 1656–1661. Of Dr. Stephen Charnock, who flourished between A.D. 1650–1680: In his work on

"The Attributes of God," he stoutly maintains, not the destruction, but the restitution of the world, inanimate, irrational, and rational, which is a cardinal point in the millenarian scheme. Also of Dr. Matthew Henry, who flourished between A.D. 1685 and 1714. On Romans 8:19–23, he says: "At the second coming of Christ, there will be a manifestation of the children of God. Now, the saints are God's hidden ones, the wheat seems lost in a heap of chaff; but then they shall be manifested...All the curse and filth that now adheres to the creature shall be done away then, when those that have suffered with Christ upon earth, shall reign with Christ upon earth. This the whole creation looks and longs for." And, on Luke 12:45, 46, he writes: "Our looking at Christ's second coming as at a distance,"—the very attitude and sin of the Church generally of this day—"is the cause of all those irregularities which render the thought of it terrible to us."

Of those whose chiliastic tenets were of a more decided cast, we may reckon John Davenant, bishop of Salisbury, A.D. 1630. John H. Alstead, an erudite professor of divinity and philosophy in Transylvania, A.D. 1627, in his "Prophetical work," affirmed that a majority of the divines of his day held that "the last judgment was even at the doors." Dr. Prideaux, about A.D. 1670, admits that the Dissenters of his day took the word "souls," Revelation 20:4, as meaning "souls and bodies united," which is purely chiliastic. Tillinghast, in A.D. 1665, taught that the second coming of Christ was but "a little way from the door." Thomas Beverly, in A.D. 1687, maintained the doctrine of a literal first resurrection, and expected a millennium to follow. The Baptists, in their confession of faith presented to Charles

II in A.D. 1660 signed by 41 elders (among which names was enrolled the world-renowned John Buyan), deacons, and approved by more than 20,000 others, was thoroughly millenarian. Dr. William Ames, of Norfolk, England, A.D. 1641; John Cocceius, professor of theology at Bremen, A.D. 1650; John Howe, A.D. 1660; and Dr. Cressener, who wrote a work in A.D. 1690 on the "Protestant Applications of the Apocalypse," were pre-millennialists.

We come now to consider, briefly, the history of millenarianism during the eighteenth century. At the opening of this century, Peter Jurieu, who flourished between A.D. 1660 and 1713, and who was styled "the Goliath of Protestantism," and who for the most part followed Mr. Mede as his master, writes that "many divines in this country (England) have greatly murmured at it (i.e., millenarianism), even so far as to threaten to complain of me. I am sorry for it, for I should be glad not to displease my brethren." This shows that the spirit of hostility to these tenets must have been of an exceedingly virulent character, thus to have intimidated even this "Goliath of Protestantism." But, as we shall see, the present age is not unfruitful of a similar class of millenarian "Goliaths" among ourselves.

The following expounders and advocates of chiliasm, however, appeared upon the stage about this time, in both hemispheres. Robert Fleming, the son of a Scotch minister, was the great grandson of the celebrated John Knox, on his mother's side. A pious and learned divine, he was the pastor first of the Leyden and Rotterdam churches, and afterward of the Presbyterian church in Lothbury, Scotland. Besides other works, he is the author of the remarkable treatise of *The Rise and Fall of the Papacy*, published first in A.D. 1701. He fixed the date of the former event at A.D. 552, Julian time, from which, however, he deducted 18 years, to accommodate this date to prophetical time, thus making the "rise" of the Papacy to correspond with A.D. 533, when, by the edict of Justinian I, John II, the then bishop of Rome, was constituted the universal head of all the Churches in Christendom. From this date, by the addition of the 1260 years of Daniel 7:25, he placed the period of its "fall" at A.D. 1794 (or rather 1793). The astonishing accuracy of this date was verified in those signal judgments which took effect upon the Papal power during the troubles of the first French Revolution, when Louis XVI, king of France, was beheaded, and the Robespierrean "Reign of Terror" commenced, a circumstance which, when remembered, produced a most thrilling sensation throughout Great Britain. Not that that event was to complete the destruction of the Papacy under the fifth vial, "though it would exceedingly weaken it." Its final overthrow awaited the effusion of the seventh vial. But Mr. Fleming was less happy in his adjustment of the chronology of events connected with the seals, trumpets, and vials of the Apocalypse. This arose from his having overlooked that important discrepancy in the chronology of the Old Testament between 1 Kings 6:1 and Acts 13:17–22, relating to the period from the Exode [departure from Egypt] to the fourth year of Solomon, in consequence of which, by the addition of 2,000 years to A.M. 4004, in order to complete the 6000 years, he carried that period beyond the A.D. 1793 to the extent of 207 years. At the same time, he observes, "Seeing the 1260 days (or years) are the whole time of the Papal authority, it is not to be totally destroyed until the great and remarkable appearance of Christ, upon the pouring out of the seventh vial; and that, therefore, Christ will have the honor of destroying him finally Himself (though this iniquity began to work in the apostolic times); wherefore, we may certainly conclude...that though the Lord will gradually consume or waste this great adversary by the spirit of his mouth, yet he will not sooner abolish him than by the appearance of His own presence." (2 Thessalonians 2:8). And again: speaking of the seventh vial being poured out on the air, he says: "As Christ concluded his sufferings on the cross with this voice, 'It is finished;' so the Church's sufferings are concluded with the voice out of the temple of heaven, 'It is done.' And therefore, with this doth the blessed millennium of Christ's spiritual reign on earth begin." These extracts from Mr. Fleming's work are decidedly millenarian.

Contemporaneous with this writer was the renowned Sir Isaac Newton, who flourished between A.D. 1665–1727. Of his millenarianism it is unnecessary to enlarge. "His praise," as such, is, or should be, "in all the Churches."

Increase Mather, D.D., was born in Dorchester, Massachusetts, in A.D. 1639. He was minister of the North Church in Boston for 62 years, which included 15 years presidency of Harvard College. From his biographer, we learn that he became a student of prophecy, and when made aware that the early Church, till the fourth century, taught the pre-millennial advent and kingdom of Christ on earth, "he found himself under the necessity of becoming a sober chiliast." He furnishes a synopsis of his millenarian views in a work entitled the *Remarkables of Mather's Life*, which Mather himself fully verifies in his *Mystery of Salvation*, published in A.D. 1668, and also in his sermon on Titus 2:13. His biographer adds: that "he mightily looked up to heaven for direction and assistance in all his inquiries into the character and approaches of the holy kingdom," and that, "by studying the prophecies, and meditating upon the paradisiacal state which will then be at the restitution of all things, he sailed so near to the land of promise, that he felt the balsamic breezes of the heavenly country upon his mind."

This, however, we suppose, is rather too "materializing," "gross," and "sensual," to suit the refined tastes of the modern school of allegorists. Thus it was at the opening of this eighteenth century. The teachings of a Fleming and a Sir Isaac Newton in England and Scotland, and of a Mather in America, did not avail to prevent the introduction of a new era in the department of prophetical exposition. For this, the Church is indebted to Dr. Daniel Whitby, who flourished between A.D. 1660–1680. He himself styles his millennial theory "A New Hypothesis." Yes, an hypothesis, i,e., a system that is founded on conjecture, or an opinion, or something supposed but not proved: directly the opposite of a thesis, which is defined to be a proposition, a position, a statement. Well, let us see what this "New Hypothesis" is. Bishop Russell, who is an impartial witness (being himself an anti-millenarian), says: "For example, the phrase, 'coming of Christ,' which in former times conveyed the most exalted ideas in respect to the destinies of the world, is conventionally employed in our day to mean the hour of every individual's death. The first resurrection, according to Whitby and his followers, implies nothing more than the conversion of the Jews; the reign of the saints with the

Redeemer a thousand years on earth, denotes simply the revival of evangelical doctrine; and by the rest of the dead we are to understand a generation of bad men, who are to be born about the end of the millennium, and to appear to annoy the congregation of the faithful. Those very persons who were not to have fathers or mothers for 900 years afterward, are, agreeably to this "hypothesis," described as the rest of the dead, at the moment the martyrs were raised to live and reign with Christ...Every person who reads the Book of Revelation without any bias on his mind, and then turns to the far-fetched commentaries of Dr. Whitby and his pupils, will perceive either that undue liberties have been used by them in expounding the original, or that John the Divine did not know the meaning of his own words."

Nor this only. Take the following, from Dr. Whitby himself, which, says the *London Quarterly Journal* for A.D. 1850, "comes to us with the weight of an irresistible testimony" in condemnation of his own "New Hypothesis." In his "Treatise on Tradition," he says: "The doctrine of the millennium, or the reign of saints for 1000 years, is now rejected by all Roman Catholics, and by the greatest part of Protestants; and yet it passed among the best Christians for 250 years for a tradition apostolical; and as such is delivered by many fathers of the second and third centuries, who spake of it as the tradition of our Lord and His apostles, and of all the ancients that lived before them; who tell us the very words in which it was delivered, the Scriptures, which were then so interpreted, and say that it was held by all Christians who were exactly orthodox." Then, quoting the fathers in proof, he sums up with the following statements: "It was received not only in the eastern parts of the Church by Papias (in Phrygia), Justin (in Palestine), Irenaeus (in Gaul), Nepos (in Egypt), Apollinarius, Methodius (in the west and south), Cyprian, Victorious (in Germany), by Tertullian (in Africa), Lactantius (in Italy), and Severus, and by the Council of Nice," i.e., in A.D. 323. And he continues: "These men taught this doctrine, not as doctors only, but as witnesses of the tradition which they had received from Christ and His apostles, and which was taught by the elders, the disciples of Christ. They pretend to ground it upon numerous and manifest testimonies both of the Old and New Testaments, and speak of them as texts which admit of no other meaning."

Now, in view of the universally admitted rule of Tertullian in these premises, that "whatever is first, is true, whatever is later, is adulterate;" what are we to think of those modern writers "whose respect for everything Catholic and apostolic," like that of "Eusebius," is declared to be "very high," yet ignore the testimony of such a cloud of "witnesses" in behalf of primitive chiliasm, and substitute in its place "the far-fetched" "New Hypothesis" of Dr. Whitby? Yes, and that in the face of the following statement of Archdeacon Woodhouse, a decided post-millennialist, who justly observes: "It is remarkable that Dr. Whitby, who had declined to comment on the Apocalypse, assigning as his motive, that he felt himself unqualified for such a work, has ventured to explain this particular prediction of the millennium (i.e., Revelation 20:4–6, on which his entire theory is founded), which being, as all agree, a prophecy yet unfulfilled, is, of all others, the most difficult!"

It is, however, nevertheless a fact, that during this eighteenth century, "the greatest part of Protestants of this day, as Dr. Whitby affirms of his own times, have endorsed this "far-fetched" and novel "hypothesis" of that writer! But we affirm that, in spite of the professed "orthodoxy" of these "Protestants," by whatsoever name they may be called, at this very point the great boundary line is drawn, which demonstrates the apostasy of the modern Church from that cardinal "faith" regarding the second personal coming of the Lord "at first delivered to the saints" by the ancient patriarchs and prophets, and by Christ and the New Testament writers! Its principal advocates since the time of Whitby have been Hopkins, Scott, Dwight, Bougue and others. But we herewith confidently challenge the production of any one writer in its defense before the commencement of this eighteenth century. Will the Churches heed it?

It may here be in place to state, that the Rev. Alexander Pirie, of Newburgh, Scotland, a stanch millenarian, about A.D. 1700, controverted the statement of "Dr. Whitby and his numerous followers, that a proper and literal resurrection is never in the whole New Testament expressed or represented by the living of the soul, but by the living, raising, and resurrection of the dead—the rising of the bodies of the saints." Pirie, quoting the prophecy of David by Peter, concerning Christ, that "His soul was not left in hell (hades), neither did His flesh see corruption" (Acts 2:27–31); having argued that "here is a proper and literal resurrection expressed in the New Testament, by the living again of the soul;" and that, "as the resurrection of the first-born from the dead is so expressed," that it was "proper to express the resurrection of his younger brethren in the same way," he adds: "When we hear John saying,

'I saw the souls of them that were beheaded, and they lived and reigned with Christ a thousand years,' we must necessarily understand this as spoken of their reanimated and risen bodies, because Peter has taught us so to explain the resurrection of the soul of Christ, the Lord and Head of the resurrection." "Besides," he continues, "how could John see a soul separated from the body?" He hence concluded that "the above remark of Dr. Whitby is unfounded in truth." What say the Whitbyites?

It is not, however, to be supposed that the light of millenarianism expired with Pirie. Throughout this entire century, England, Scotland, and America have produced numerous advocates of it, who have shone among the brightest luminaries in the ecclesiastical firmament.

Arranging these in their chronological order, we begin with Cotton Mather, D.D., a son of Increase Mather, already noticed. He succeeded his father as minister of the North Church, Boston, and was the most distinguished and learned clergyman of his day in New England. His writings are numerous, the most celebrated of which is his *Magnalia*. Like his father, he was an eminent chiliast. All its cardinal tenets are fully exhibited in his work entitled *The Student and Preacher, or Directions for a Candidate of the Ministry*. Edmund Wells, professor of Greek in Oxford, in A.D. 1720, was a decided millenarian. Charles Daubuz, of France, a scholar of the first rank, published an Apocalyptic commentary in A.D. 1720, which is pronounced to be "the ablest of all the commentaries on the visions of St. John." He mainly followed Mede and Jurieu, and maintains throughout the purest chiliastic tenets. John Albert Begel, of Wurtemberg, Germany, A.D. 1720. He is celebrated as a prophetical writer, and united in himself, as Dr. Adam Clarke affirms, "the deepest piety and the most extensive learning." His "memoirs and writings show him to be thoroughly millenarian." Dr. Isaac Watts's Psalms and Hymns abound in the doctrines of the personal advent, the literal resurrection of the saints, the terrestrial reign, the recreation of the earth, and the descent of the New Jerusalem. It may truly be said that "Watts has sung in noblest strains of the bright hope of a fallen, ruined world." Joseph Perry, of Northampton, England, in his work called *The Glory of Christ's Visible Kingdom in this World*, published in A.D. 1721, he lucidly sets forth the pre-millennial reign of Christ and His saints.

William Lowth, distinguished as a theologian and commentator, A.D. 1730, was a chiliast. See his commentary on Ezekiel 11:23; 43:2; Daniel 7:9, and verse 27. Sayer Rudd, M.D., London, wrote an *Essay on the Resurrection, Millennium, and Judgment*, which was published in A.D. 1734, and in which he confuted, in a masterly manner, as a pre-millennialist, the theory of Whitby. Joseph Hussey, an author of some distinction, in Cambridge, A.D. 1730, wrote a work entitled *The Glories of Christ*. He was a most decided millenarian. Robert Hort, A.M., chaplain to his grace Josiah, Lord Archbishop of Tuam, in A.D. 1747, was an able advocate of chiliasm.

Dr. John Gill, also, who flourished between A.D. 1750–1771, was a Baptist, and rose to high eminence as a divine, theologian, and orientalist. All who are conversant with his extensive Prophetical Sermons, Body of Divinity, and Commentary, are aware that he was a thorough millenarian. Would not our Baptist brethren of this day do well to call to mind the millenarianism of good old Bunyan and the

20,000 brethren of his time, and also that of their great Dr.
Gill, of whom they may be so justly proud?

We now come to the time of the Wesleys and of
Fletcher, who flourished between A.D. 1723 and 1788. John
Wesley was a decided millenarian. His views on this subject
may be found in his published works (New York ed.), vol.
5, and vol. 6, and also in his *Notes on the New Testament*,
published in A.D. 1754. See his comments on Matthew
24:36, and 2 Peter 3:12. As it respects the Apocalypse, while
he does not "pretend to understand or explain all that is
contained in this mysterious book," yet he remarks that
it "reaches from the Old Jerusalem to the New," and also
that the seven trumpets extend "nearly from the time of
St. John to the end of the world;" by which he meant, not
the end of time, but this age or dispensation, for, he says,
the dominion of Christ appears in an entirely new manner,
as soon as the seventh angel sounds." Again: while he says
that "some have miserably handled this book," he severely
rebukes those who "are afraid to touch it...They inquire
after anything rather than this, as if it were written, 'Happy
is he that doth not read this prophecy;'" to which he says,
"Nay, but happy is he that readeth," Revelation 1:3...And
then adds "It behooves every Christian at all opportunities
to read what is written in the oracles of God, and to read
this precious book in particular, frequently, reverently, and
attentively; for the time is near—even when St. John wrote.
How much nearer to us is even the full accomplishment of
this weighty prophecy!" See also comments on Revelation
5:4; and chapters 14–22. This eminent divine, and the
founder of Methodism, evidently adopts the main tenets of
the early chiliastic fathers, but in interpreting the Revelation,

like Bengel, whose views he adopted for the most part, he singularly gathers two millenniums from Revelation 20:1–6: the first, "a flourishing state of the Church on earth;" the second, "a reign of the saints with Christ in heaven," allowing verse 6 to teach a literal resurrection of the martyrs and saints. This, however, arose from a confounding of things which differ, a peculiarity of many of the writers both before and after his time. We would only add, that Mr. Wesley fully endorsed Mr. Hartley's book, called *Paradise Restored: a Testimony to the Doctrine of the blessed Millennium*, a book wholly and positively millenarian, being written expressly in defense of it.

We here introduce to the notice of the reader the name of John Fletcher, vicar of Madely, an associate of Mr. Wesley, a most pious and learned man, a close student of the prophecies, and a stanch millenarian. He addressed a "Letter on the Prophecies" to Mr. Wesley, dated A.D. 1775, in which he refers to a certain "great and learned man," who, with Sir Isaac Newton, held that we are come to the last times," and that Christ was coming to destroy the wicked, and raise the righteous dead a thousand years before the final judgment. These views Mr. Fletcher fully endorses, and proceeds in said letter and in his other writings to elucidate them at considerable length; and, on the subject of the chronology of "the time of the end" (Daniel 12:9), he reaches a conclusion nearly coincident with the most reliable writers of the present day. " If," he says, "Jesus told his disciples that it was not theirs to know the times when these things should be accomplished, it does not follow that it must be hid from us who are far nearer concerned in them than they were." And he adds: "I know many have been grossly mistaken as to the years; but because they were rash, shall we be stupid? Because they said 'today,' shall we say 'never,' and cry 'peace, peace,' when we should look about us with eyes full of expectation?" And then, exhorting us "to hasten by our prayers that glorious kingdom," and adding the exclamation, "What a glorious prospect is this!" he says: "Let us then often think of our Lord. 'Behold I come quickly.' Blessed is he that mindeth the sayings of this prophecy. Let us join 'the Spirit and the Bride,' who say, 'come.' Oh, 'let him that heareth say, come; and let him that is athirst, come; for he that testifieth these things saith, Surely I come quickly. Amen: even so, come, Lord Jesus!'"

That Charles Wesley's views coincided with those of John on these subjects, is evident from his numerous hymns, in which he shows great familiarity with millenarian doctrines, and refers frequently to them as topics of warm personal expectation. Thus, on the text, "I know that my Redeemer liveth," he says:

> "Jesus shall reappear below,
> Stand in that dreadful day unknown,
> *And fix on earth His heavenly throne.*"

On Isaiah 39:23, he represents the Savior as proclaiming His glorious advent and the setting up of His future kingdom, thus:

> "Then, Sion, thou shalt fully know
> The King of kings revealed below.
> In glorious majesty Divine,

Expecting Me on earth to reign,
My people shall not wait in vain."

On Isaiah 60:13, he sings in the same strain:

"That place where once I walked below,
   On Olivet, I will appear:
My bleeding feet to Israel show,
   While those who pierced, behold me near
Again I will forsake My throne,
   And to My footstool earth descend:
And fill the world with peace unknown,
   With glorious joy, that ne'er shall end."

So, on Isaiah 65:17, he prays:

"Come, Divine, effectual power,
Fallen nature to restore:
Wait we for Thy presence here,
Lord, to see Thy throne appear;
Bid the new creation rise,
Bring us back our Paradise.
"Now our universe create,
Fair beyond its first estate,
When Thine eyes with pleasure viewed,
When Thy lips pronounced it good:
Ruined now by sin, and curst,
Speak it fairer than at first."

Thus, again, he celebrates the restoration of the literal
Israel in the latter day:

"We know it must be done,
    For God hath spoke the word;
All Israel shall their Savior own,
    To their first state restored.
Rebuilt by His command,
    Jerusalem shall rise;
Her temple on Moriah stand
    Again, and touch the skies."

And his continuation of the same theme is equally clear and decisive:

"When the house of Jacob's sons
    Their Canaan repossess,
Shall not all thy chosen ones
    Abide in perfect peace?
Trusting in the literal word,
    We look for Christ on earth again;
Come, our everlasting Lord,
    With all Thy saints to reign!"

Again:

"When wilt Thou on Thy throne appear,
Triumphant with Thine ancients here!"

Again:

"Lord, as taught by Thee, we pray
    That sin and death may end;
In the great millennial day,

With all thy saints descend."

Again:

"Dismissed, I calmly go my way,
    Which leads me to the tomb;
And rest in hope of that great day,
    When my desire shall come.
Happy *with those that first arise,*
    Might I my lot obtain,
When Christ, descending from the skies,
    Begins His glorious reign."

It is plainly not a spiritual reign alone, but a personal one, preceded by the resurrection of the just only, which he here anticipates, as the following also shows:

"Come, my God, Jehovah, come,
    With all Thy saints appear;
Antichrist expects his doom,
    And we, Thy kingdom here.
Thee, Jesus, Lord of lords we know,
    The kingdoms of the earth are Thine;
Hasten t' erect *Thy throne below,*
    That last great monarchy divine."

The same is embraced in his hymns on Malachi, where he also asserts his belief that Elijah is yet to reappear on the earth, to testify again for the living God:

"*Once he in the Baptist came,*

And virtue's path restored;
   Pointed sinners to the Lamb
      Forerunner of his Lord.
Sent again from Paradise,
   Elijah shall the tidings bring:
"Jesus comes! ye saints arise,
      And meet your Heavenly King."

Again:

"Previous to the dreadful day,
   Which shall Thy foes consume;
Jesus, to prepare Thy way,
   Let the last prophet come.
When the seventh trumpet's sound
   Proclaims the grand sabbatic year:
Come Thyself, with glory crowned,
   And reign triumphant here."

Come, then, our Heavenly Friend,
   Sorrow and death to end;
Pure millennial joy to give,
   Now appear on earth again:
Now thy people, saved, receive,
   Now begin thy glorious reign."

"Before the final general doom,
We know Thou wilt to judgment come;
Thy foes destroy, Thy friends maintain,
And glorious with Thine ancients reign."

And yet once more sings this prolific and often enrapturing songster:

> "Mightier joys ordained to know,
> *When Thou com'st to reign below.*
> We shall at Thy side sit down,
> Partners of Thy great white throne;
> Kings a thousand years with Thee,
> Kings through all eternity."

Do the admirers and followers of these Wesleys and Fletchers think that these devout and able men were altogether in error on these topics? Are they prepared to take issue with their own greatest authorities and leaders? Have they learned the Scriptures better than these through whom they have been taught the way to heaven, and by whom their songs before the face of God in His sanctuary are led? We find many of our Methodist and Wesleyan contemporaries very strongly adverse to millenarian doctrines, and unwilling even to entertain the subject for examination. Will they please tell us what they think of their fathers in these matters? Will they bear with us in quoting for them the admonition of the prophet: "Stand ye in the ways, and see, and ask for the old paths, and walk therein; and ye shall find rest for your souls?" (See Prophetical Times, Vol. ii, No. 9).

Dr. George Benson, an eminent Dissenting divine in England, from A.D. 1750 to 1763, in his notes on Psalm 96:10–13, and 98:4–9, is clearly millenarian. Here also looms up a Roman Catholic ecclesiastic in France, Francis Lambert, who flourished between A.D. 1750 and 1763, the author of a work on the prophecies, first published in Paris, 1806, in which, contrary to the doctrines of his Church, he gives a striking testimony in favor of millennial views. In this work, having spoken at length upon the punishments which were to fall on apostate Gentiles—among whom he includes Roman Catholic nations as well as Protestant—and dividing them into three periods, which the Scriptures call worlds, the first, the antediluvian, which perished by the flood; the second, from Noah to the close of this corrupted world (or age), respecting which our Lord said to Pilate, "My kingdom is not of this world;" he adds, "in fine, the third, which is yet future, is that which the apostle calls 'the world to come;" or (Greek) 'the habitable earth to come.'" Hebrews 2:5. Allowing for some errors in his details, the above is a tolerably fair exposition of chiliasm. Thomas Prince, pastor of the Old South Church, Boston, Massachusetts, from A.D. 1728 to 1758, of whom Chauncey said, "he was second in learning to none but Cotton Mather," was an eminent pre-millennialist. John Glas, of Scotland, whose works consist of four volumes, published in Edinburgh, A.D. 1761, show him to have been a strong advocate of chiliasm. N. Lancaster, D.D., A.D. 1770, was a pre-millenarian.

The next distinguished writer of this century is Augustus M. Toplady, À.D. 1765 and 1778. The following declaration, besides what appears in his voluminous writings, sufficiently attests his millenarianism. He says: "I am one of those old-fashioned people who believe the doctrine of the millennium, and that there will be two distinct resurrections of the dead: first, of the just, and second, of the unjust; which last resurrection of the reprobate will not commence till a thousand years after the resurrection of the elect. In this glorious interval of a thousand years, Christ, I apprehend, will reign in person over the kingdom of the just; and that during this dispensation (i.e., the millennial), different degrees of glory will obtain, and every man shall receive his own reward according to his own labor."

Thomas Newton, D.D., bishop of Bristol, England, from A.D. 1725 to 1784, the well-known author of *Newton's Dissertations on the Prophecies*. That he was a millenarian, is evident from the following: "Nothing is more evident," he observes, "than that this prophecy of the millennium, and of the first resurrection, (meaning that of Revelation 20:1– 6) hath not yet been fulfilled, even though the resurrection be taken in a figurative sense." And he argues: "If the martyrs rise only in a spiritual sense, then the rest of the dead rise only in a spiritual sense; but if the rest of the dead really rise, the martyrs rise in the same manner. There is no difference between them, and we should be cautious and tender of making the first resurrection an allegory, lest others should reduce the second into allegory too, like Hymeneus and Philetus." From these premises he draws the conclusion—"that the kingdom of heaven shall be established upon earth, is the plain and express doctrine of Daniel, and all the prophets, as well as of St. John; and we daily pray for the accomplishment of it in praying, 'Thy kingdom come.'"

William Newcome, the eminently learned archbishop of Armagh, Ireland, A.D. 1780 to 1799, on Revelation 20:4, he says: "I understand this not figuratively of a peaceable and flourishing state of the Church on earth, but literally of a real resurrection, and of a real reign with Christ, who will display His royal glory in the New Jerusalem. This is the great sabbatism or rest of the Church."

Dr. B. Gale, of Killingworth, Connecticut, from A.D. 1725 to 1795. He was a laborious student of the prophecies. John W. Barber, in his *Historical Collections of Connecticut,* in a comment on his epitaph, says: "It appears by this inscription, that Dr. Gale was a believer in the ancient doctrine of millenarians, a name given to those who believe that the second coming of Christ will precede the millennium, and that there will be a literal resurrection of the saints, who will reign with Christ on earth a thousand years. This appears to have been the belief of pious persons at the time of the first settlement of New England. Even as late as the great earthquake, 1775, many Christians were looking for and expecting the second coming of Christ."

William Cowper, England's "Christian poet," of imperishable fame, flourished from about A.D. 1756 to 1800. A thorough millenarian, in his *Task* he has sung in glorious numbers of the signs of the times, the world's age, the second coming of the Lord, the restitution of all things, the reign of Christ and his saints on earth, the New Jerusalem, and of all those "scenes surpassing fable" but just before us:

"The world appears
To toll the death-bell of its own decease—
...The old
And crazy earth has had her shaking fits
More frequent, and foregone her usual rest;
And nature seems with dim and sickly eye
To wait the close of all,

Six thousand years of sorrow have well nigh
Fulfilled their tardy and disastrous course
Over a sinful world : and what remains
Of this tempestuous state of human things,
Is merely as the rocking of a sea
Before a calm that rocks itself to rest.

Behold the measure of the promise filled;
See Salem built, the labor of a God!
Bright as a sun the Sacred City shines:
All kingdoms and all princes of the earth
Flock to that light: the glory of all lands
Flows into her; unbounded is her joy,
And endless her increase.

Come then, and added to Thy many crowns,
Receive yet one, the crown of all the earth,
For Thou alone art worthy.
Thy saints proclaim Thee King; and Thy delay
Gives courage to their foes, who, could they see
The dawn of Thy last advent, long desired,
Would flee for safety to the falling rocks."

That the eminently learned theologian and divine, William Romaine, who flourished between about A.D. 1736 and 1795, could not have embraced the Whitbyan theory, is evident from the following: he writes—"The marks and signs of Christ's second advent are fulfilling daily. His coming cannot be far off. If you compare the uncommon events which the Lord said were to be the forerunners of his coming to judgment, with what hath lately happened in the world, you must conclude the time is at hand."

Joshua Spaulding was minister of the Gospel at the Tabernacle in Salem, Massachusetts, A.D. 1796. The "Lectures" of this pious and able divine, which are well known, abundantly attest his advocacy of the millenarian tenets. We have already spoken of the Rev. Robert Hall, a Baptist minister and writer of great talent, and one of the most eloquent and extraordinary men of his time. That he was a millenarian, is testified to by Mr. Thorp, of Bristol, England (himself an able advocate of that doctrine), certifying that he fully avowed himself to be such in a conversation with him on the subject a few days before his death, but, like some others, hid his light under a bushel, which he greatly regretted on his dying bed. Dr. Thomas Coke, LL.D., an associate of the Wesleys, was a thorough chiliast. In his Commentary he follows and quotes Mede, Daubuz, Newton, and others, firmly advocating the pre-millennial view of the second coming of our Lord. We close the above partial galaxy of witnesses "for the word of God and the testimony which they held" in behalf of the truth, with the name of Reginald Heber.

Reginald Heber, the eminently pious bishop of Calcutta, distinguished alike as a divine and poet. He died suddenly at Trichinopoly in India, A.D. 1826. His millenarianism stands out in bold relief in many of his poètical effusions and other writings. We limit ourself, however, to the following extract from his spirited poem, "Palestine," which gained for him the prize at Oxford:

"And who is He? the vast, the awful form (Revelation 10:1, 2),

Girt with the whirlwind, sandall'd with the storm!
A western cloud around his limbs is spread,
His crown a rainbow, and the sun his head.
To highest heaven he lifts his kingly hand,
And treads at once the ocean and the land:
And hark! His voice amidst the thunders roar,
His dreadful voice, that time shall be no more.
Lo! thrones are set, and every saint is there.
(Revelation 20:4–6)
Earth's utmost bounds confess their awful sway,
The mountains worship, and the isles obey:
Nor sun, nor moon they need—nor day, nor night;
God is their temple, and the Lamb their light
(Revelation 21:22);
And shall not Israel's sons exulting come,
Hail the glad beam and claim their ancient home?
On David's throne shall David's offspring reign,
And the dry bones be warm with life again. (Ezekiel
27)
Hark! white-robed crowds their deep hosannas
raise,
And the hoarse flood resounds the sound of praise;
Ten thousand harps attune the mystic song,
Ten thousand thousand saints the strain prolong!
Worthy the Lamb, omnipotent to save,
Who died, who lives triumphant o'er the grave."

CONCLUSION

Hall (a Baptist), and Thorp (an Independent), and Coke (a Methodist), and Heber (an Episcopalian), formed a sort of quadruple millenarian link, between the close of the eighteenth and the opening of the nineteenth centuries. That talented French divine and master of eloquence, John B. Massillon, who died in A.D. 1742, while he admits that in the first ages it would have been deemed a kind of apostasy not to have sighed after "the day of the Lord," yet says it was very difficult in his day, on account of the worldly minded and lukewarm state of the Church, "to call up the minds of the people to attend to the subject of the Lord's advent." Dr. Gill, too, testifies that the Churches in this (the eighteenth) century, had a name to live, and were dead: "a sleepy frame of spirit," he says, "having seized upon us, both ministers and Churches are asleep." Bengel also called it "a poor, slumbering age, that needed an awakener."

Such was the complaint, both in England and on the Continent. And there was a cause for this coldness. Whitby had lived and wrote, and his "New Hypothesis," by which the personal coming of the Lord is necessarily postponed for 1,000 years, had stifled the warning note of, "Behold, I come quickly." That "belief in the speedy advent of the Savior and habitual contemplation of the last things, which adds weight and impressiveness to the ordinary preaching of the Gospel, giving it earnestness, fervor, and solemnity not often attained," was now getting unpopular, and, as in the fourth century, truth measurably dimmed before widespread error, and, with the decay of pre-millennialism, spiritual life, too, died away.

Such then was the disastrous effect resulting from the prevalence of the Whitbyan "New Hypothesis" in England and on the Continent at the opening of the nineteenth century. But, thank God, in that extensive field, and especially in Great Britain—and of which England is the principal seat—within the last half century, and particularly within the last 25 years, many of the leading pulpit orators, or who are so regarded by the mass of the people, are the decided advocates of the millenarian doctrine of the speedy personal coming of Christ, and his reign upon the earth. Hundreds of voices and of pens, in the pulpit and through the press, have been and are still engaged in their endeavors to rescue the Church from the delusion of the Whitbyan theory, and to recover her to the acceptance and belief of those truths of the New Testament and early post-apostolic times, for which so many millions of martyrs bled and died. Many of the pulpits in Great Britain are employed in raising "the midnight cry, behold the bridegroom cometh, go ye out to meet him." Nor are these pulpits confined to one class only. They are occupied by scores of the clergy of the established Churches of nearly equal celebrity, but of whom Dr. Elliott, Dean Alvord, Dr. Margoliouth, Dr. Tregelles, Dr. Hugh McNeile, and Dr. Ryle, take the lead. In the Scotch Church, besides many others, are Dr. Bonar and Dr. Cumming, the latter one of the most voluminous and eloquent writers of the age. Then there are the Rev. Mr. Spurgeon and the Rev. Mr. Cox, of the Baptist Church; and the Rev. Denham Smith, of the Independents. Nearly all of these have also employed their pens in the same cause, thus placing themselves in the ranks of the most eminently learned and extensive writers of the day. In addition to these may be added, among the most recent authors in defense of millenarianism, the following: Rev. Dr. French, Rev. W. Wood, Rev. E. Nangle, Rev. Wm. Harker, Rev. E. Auriol, Rev. C. I. Goodhart, Rev. Dr. Leask, Rev. Mr. Chester, Rev. A. Dallas, Rev. E. Gillson, Rev. T.R. Berks, Rev. James Kelly,

Rev. J.G. Gregory, Rev. C. Molineux, Rev. David Pitcairn, Rev. Frederic Fysh, M.A., George Ogilvie, Esq. There are also large numbers of books and tracts issued by several of the leading publishing houses in London. Among these may be noted Wm. McIntosh, Paternoster Row; S.W. Partridge; James Nesbitt & Co., Bernners Street; and Wm. Yapp, Walbeck Street. And to these may be added several periodicals devoted to the same cause, among which are, "The Quarterly Journal of Prophecy," edited by Dr. Bonar; and "The Rainbow," an interesting and sprightly monthly, edited by Dr. Leask.

This augurs well for the cause on the other side of the Atlantic. The Churches there have been aroused from that "poor, slumbering" state, as Bengel expresses it, into which "a worldly-minded and lukewarm" spirit had involved them, and the minds of the people have been awakened to attend to the subject of the Lord's second coming as near at hand.

With the American Churches, however, it is otherwise. The state of the Churches as described of the times of Bengel, Massillon, and Dr. Gill, on this momentous subject, is, to a lamentable extent, applicable to our own times. We have only to refer, I submit, to what Professor Shedd says of the alleged circumstance under which the Church has been recovered to his so-called "Catholic theory of the second advent," to obtain a clue to the cause of this state of things. Speaking of the Church in the time of Constantine, he says: "The pressure of persecution being lifted off, the Church returned to its earlier and first exegesis of the Scripture data concerning the end of the world, and the second coming of Christ...The personal coming of Christ, it was now held, is not to take place until the final day of doom." But we have demonstrated that nothing is further removed from the truth than this. Why, what said the covenant God of Israel to his chosen people? "Behold, I have refined thee, but not with silver: I have chosen thee in the furnace of affliction. For mine own sake, even for mine own sake, I will do it." (Isaiah 48:10, 11). And what did Jesus say concerning his followers? "In the world ye shall have tribulation." (John 16:33. See also Acts 14:22). And of the redeemed in "the world to come" it is said, "These are they which came out of great tribulation," (Revelation 7:14). As, therefore, it was not "persecution" which made the early post-apostolic martyrs chiliasts; so, just in proportion as persecution was "lifted off" from the Church, and the tide of worldly prosperity and its concomitants set in, did she adopt, not, as Professor Shedd affirms, the "earlier and first exegesis of the Scripture data concerning the end of the world and the second coming of Christ," but the unscriptural theory of Augustine.

And so, we now affirm that, just in proportion as a similar tide of worldly prosperity and exemption from suffering for Christ's sake has marked the progress of the American Churches,—Episcopal, Presbyterian, Dutch Reformed, Methodist, and Baptist—while they have ignored the ancient Augustinian theory, they have adopted the equally unscriptural and, as Bishop Russell of Scotland styles it, the "far-fetched" "New Hypothesis" of Dr. Whitby; which, removing that great event, the second personal coming of Christ, at least 1000 years hence, or, as the learned Professor states it, "until the final day of doom," they have settled down into "a poor, frigid, slumbering" state—that very state indicated by the "five foolish virgins" in the parable—

regarding that crisis! We repeat: that "belief in the speedy advent of the Savior and habitual contemplation of the last things, which adds weight and impressiveness to the ordinary preaching of the gospel, giving it earnestness, fervor, and solemnity not often attained" (we quote from the New York Independent for A.D. 1850), by having been rendered unpopular, has nearly died out. The Whitbyan "New Hypothesis" holds the decided predominance among us over both the clergy and the laity. Alas, over the laity, because of the tenacity with which the clergy still cling to it.

Nor this only. Our duty to God compels us to advert to the fact of the consequent lamentable neglect, on the part of most of the clergy of this day, to "study to show themselves approved unto God, workmen that need not to be ashamed," in the article of that "diligent inquiring and searching into what, or what manner of time the spirit of Christ which was in the old prophets did signify, when it testified beforehand the sufferings of Christ, and the glory that should follow." The writer could give the names of not a few of the most distinguished of these, who urge the pressure of other duties in justification of their neglect in familiarizing themselves with "the teachings of Isaiah and John concerning the second coming of Christ." And this is attempted to be fortified by the plea, that the prophecies are so dark, obscure, and enigmatical, that they lay beyond the reach of ordinary scriptural "exegesis;" that the most learned and pious divines differ in their interpretations of them; that they can only be understood by us as they are fulfilled; and finally, that, as their ultimate accomplishment is removed at too great a distance to interest our inquiries, therefore, all attempts to lay open these alleged secret councils of Jehovah's will, only tend to produce unease among sober-minded Christians, and to lead to fanaticism and delusion. It is in vain we plead, in the plain and emphatic language of Peter, that "we have a more sure word of prophecy, to which we all do well that we take heed, as unto a light which shineth in a dark place, until the day dawn, and the day-star arise in our hearts." In vain that we quote that benediction, "Blessed is he that readeth, and they that hear the words of this prophecy, and keep those things which are written therein, for the time is at hand," that is, for the commenced accomplishment of "all those things which God hath spoken by the mouth of all His holy prophets since the world began."

Pardon us, therefore, reader, if we once more repeat, that it is to the wide-spread prevalence and influence of the "far-fetched" "New Hypothesis" of Dr. Whitby throughout the Churches of this land, that we are indebted for that spirit of indifference, not only, but of open and covert hostility to the cause we advocate, so generally characteristic of these "last times." And so—the assertions of some to the contrary notwithstanding—the consequence is, that "the spirit of God seems to be withdrawn from the Churches," and that "they are dead, dead, dead:" words uttered in the hearing of the writer, by two of the most distinguished pastors of Churches in this city.

At the same time, we have cause for thankfulness that some efforts have been and still are being put forth—and they are gradually assuming larger proportions—both through the pulpit and the press, to arouse the Churches in this country to a view of the coming crisis before them. As in the record already given of those bright and shining lights in the Church, ancient, medieval, and modern, who have avowed their belief in and have advocated the millenarian tenets, so with those of the present generation. Their deep piety, "in union with an intelligent and earnest orthodoxy," and the eminence of their positions in the Church of Christ, form an invulnerable shield against those shafts of invective and satire hurled against them by their opponents. Associated as they were or are with one or other of the leading evangelical Churches of Christ, furnishes the evidence that, amid the general defection of said Churches in these premises, from that "faith at first delivered to the saints," "the God of mercy has preserved a remnant according to the election of grace," as so many beacon lights to those who, with sincere hearts, "stand in the ways," that they may "see, and ask for the old paths, where is the good way," with a desire to "walk therein." Such, surely, need be neither ashamed nor afraid to pay a respectful deference to the "interpretations put upon the teachings of Isaiah and St. John concerning the second coming of Christ," by such servants of Christ as the late millenarian Bishop Henshaw, of Rhode Island, and Bishop Meade, of Virginia; nor of such living divines and theologians as Bishop Hopkins, of Vermont, Bishop McIlvaine, of Ohio, and Bishop Southgate, of this city. To these may be added, of the Episcopal Church, the Rev. S.H. Tyng, D.D., rector of St. George's, Rev. Francis Vinton, D.D., assistant minister of Trinity Church, New York City, and Rev. Edward Winthrop, Norwalk, Ohio; also Rev. Richard Newton, D.D., and Rev. William Newton, West Chester, Pennsylvania, of the same Church. Of the Old School Presbyterian Church, Rev. Robert J. Breckinridge, D.D., of

Danville,Kentucky, Rev. Robert McCartee, D.D., Yonkers, N.Y., Rev. Charles K. Imbrie, D.D., and Rev. J. Harkness, Jersey City, N.J., Rev. William Lee, Rev. Nathaniel West, and Rev. Hugh S. Carpenter, Brooklyn, and others. Of the New School Presbyterian Church, Rev. George Duffield, D.D., of Detroit, Michigan, and Rev. Robert Adair, D.D., Philadelphia. Of the Dutch Reformed Church, Rev. John Forsyth, D.D., Rev. William R. Gordon, D.D., and Rev. J.T. Demarest, D.D., New Jersey, and others. Of the Lutheran Church, Rev. Joseph A. Seiss, D.D., Philadelphia. Of the Moravian Church, Rev. Edwin E. Reinke, Philadelphia. Of the Congregational Church, Rev. Thomas Wickes, Marietta, Ohio, Rev. Henry F. Hill, Geneseo, N.Y., Rev. Alfred Bryant, Presbyterian, Niles, Michigan, Rev. J.S. Oswald, York, Pennsylvania. In all these Churches, there may be found among the laity also not a few who are avowedly millenarians. Of the most distinguished of these, may be named Mr. David N. Lord and Eleazar Lord.

Others might be added to this list, but the above are sufficient to commend this subject to the serious consideration of every candid and unbiased inquirer after truth. Most of them have employed their pens in the form of prophetical expositions and defense of primitive and modern millenarianism, and, for learning, chasteness, and eloquence of style, will compare with those of any other. The only extant journals devoted to the exposition and defense of millenarianism proper in this country—at least the only ones that we could commend as reliable— are, "The Israelite Indeed," edited by G.R. Lederer, New York City, and "The Prophetical Times," under the editorial supervision of the Rev. Drs. Seiss, Newton, Duffield, and others, published in Philadelphia.

We here close our somewhat extended reply to Professor Shedd's article on "Eschatology," or "the second coming of Christ," in connection with his historical exposition of "millenarianism, or chiliasm," ancient, medieval, and modern. We entreat one and all, and especially the clergy, to pause, and "read before they strike." The whole subject is now before them. The points at issue, scriptural and historical, are thoroughly defined. The writer holds that, viewing this matter in connection with and as applicable to these "last perilous times" in which we live, the destiny of each one for happiness or difficulty, for time and for eternity, depends upon a right understanding and acceptance or rejection of the truth in these premises. And, in whatsoever that truth consists, of this we are assured, that it is only those who rightly look for Him" (Christ) according to a "Thus saith the Lord," to whom "He will appear the second time without sin unto salvation." (See Hebrews 9:27, 28).

Finally. Seeking to imitate the faith and hope of the New Testament saints, as centered in Christ as The Coming One," may God, of His infinite mercy, stir up our hearts to "love His appearing" (2 Timothy 4:8; Titus 2:13); and to "hasten unto the coming of the day of the Lord" (2 Peter 3:12); so that "we may be accounted worthy to escape all these things that shall come to pass, and to stand before the Son of Man," (Luke 21:36) "and not be ashamed before Him at His coming" (1 John 2:28).

Rev. Dr. David E. Seip
Editor, May 2023